HYDROPONIC GARDENING MADE EASY

THE SIMPLE, EFFECTIVE, AND AFFORDABLE WAY TO
GROW YOUR OWN ORGANIC VEGETABLES AND HERBS
INDOORS YEAR-ROUND WITHOUT SOIL

SAGE COLLINS

CONTENTS

INTRODUCTION

> *The fact that I can plant a seed and it becomes a flower, share a bit of knowledge and it becomes another's, smile at someone and receive a smile in return, are to me continual spiritual experiences.*

— LEO BUSCAGLIA

As Samuel Taylor Coleridge's poem goes, "Water, water, everywhere, Nor any drop to drink." In his epic poem, *The Rime of the Ancient Mariner*, he depicts the dilemma faced by mariners who sailed across the great seas but could not make use of the immense quantity of water surrounding them (2023). Likewise, our environment is becoming overutilized; the growing population on Earth has put a strain on the availability of food and resources, and we are running out of soil and fertile land to plant more crops and vegetables. Sustainable living is becoming a priority for many, and we need to look for new ways to secure resources for future use.

This must go on for generations to ensure the availability of resources for our grandchildren and their children.

I have been a horticulture enthusiast for decades and have lived in both extremely hot and cold climates. I've found that it's difficult to practice outdoor gardening in environments where the temperatures are too high or low. Getting fresh food was so rare that I decided to use techniques that would allow me to produce fresh vegetables and herbs on my own without having to rely on the natural environment around me. This decision proved to be a great one and eventually even made it possible for me to supply fresh produce to local restaurants. My goal is to be able to grow fresh produce with the safety of our environment in mind, and one of my priorities is avoiding the use of harmful chemicals. With this book, I want to help you acquire the knowledge needed to practice gardening methods that do not cause harm to the environment but still provide a reliable source of fresh, healthy food. The way to do this is through hydroponic gardening. Each chapter will go into great detail about why hydroponic gardening is your best choice, and I will even provide some helpful visuals to deepen your understanding and inspire your own hydroponics adventure. I'll give you guidance on choosing the right location and tools for making your hydroponic garden a success and the best kinds of plants you can grow so you can start off on the right foot.

WHY HYDROPONICS?

Urban agriculture has become an important part of our society's food-growing culture, and we can make good use of it if we can incorporate more sustainable techniques into the food-growing process. Hydroponics is the best solution for sustainable living that involves growing crops with long-lasting, cost-effective methods, creating the possibility for a more sustainable future. Let's start by talking about what I mean by "sustainability." Sustainability is related to "a method of harvesting or using a resource so that the resource is not depleted or permanently damaged" (Merriam-Webster, n.d.-d). We are heading toward a huge demand for food and resources in a world where the population is estimated to reach 9.1 billion by 2050. In order to feed this growing population, we need to increase the production of resources by approximately 70% (*Hydroponics Market Size*, n.d.). But will farmers or agricultural land resources be able to meet this need? One solution is to introduce a method that provides

- cost-effective farming techniques
- environmentally friendly practices
- sustainable use of water and other resources
- easier and more efficient planting methods

Hydroponics is a method that will help farmers and agricultural enthusiasts because it

- requires 90% less water than traditional crops grown using soil
- requires one-fourth of the space needed for traditional farms
- offers the proper amount of nutrients and oxygen and a balanced pH
- does not usually require the use of pesticides or herbicides unless there is a risk of outdoor exposure
- grows two times more crops than traditional farming with soil

Hydroponic greenhouse in Iceland

Agriculture—specifically urban agricultural methods—has been a common incentive for land owners in the past for improving and growing crops by trying new methods in planting. This concept originated from the World War II period when Americans used plots called "victory gardens" to grow their vegetables. Since then, there have been more advancements in gardening fruits, vegetables, herbs, and flowers. With the introduction of hydroponics, we have learned that we can combine both methods of gardening to enhance our farming methods with the reward of cleaner, economically sound gardening that preserves resources. Urban agriculture and hydroponics are both sustainable farming methods, but the main difference is the required space and recycling of resources. When you're looking for a method that requires less space and money to grow your food, hydroponics is the best option.

The photos you see here were taken in Iceland, and although there are negative-degree temperatures in the cold winters in Iceland, there are tomatoes growing in the greenhouses with the help of geothermal energy to keep the greenhouse warm. Knutur, an agronomist, and Helena, a horticulturist, have a family business and have been growing tomatoes for a long time using geothermal energy. The geothermal energy source comes from the water hole near a local volcano when it is active. This water hole appears right below the farm. These sources make their place, Fridheimer, the best for greenhouse farming. The couple bought Fridheimer in 1995, and this greenhouse has been a good source of income ever since.

There are even some well-known celebrities who have adopted hydroponics in their gardening practices and are loving it. Nash Grier, Zoe Saldana, and Shay Mitchell are some of those who have been using methods like self-watering or self-fertilizing hydroponics. Jennie Garth is proud of her roses growing without soil or pesticides in her garden, and she's grown other plants with hydroponics. "It makes me proud to grow food… and it tastes so good!" (Hansen, 2020).

Hydroponic tomatoes growing in a greenhouse in Iceland

Hydroponics offers the option to grow plants, including vegetables, fruits, herbs, and flowers, without the trouble of creating and maintaining the right soil conditions and quality, and it omits the risk of many pathogens found in soil that can be harmful to your plants. With hydroponics, you even have the option to use vertical planting methods if you're working with limited space, such as on a rooftop or terrace.

Each chapter will show you a different aspect of this amazing gardening method that will give you and your family a great source of fresh, delicious, homegrown food all year round.

Hydroponic tomatoes growing in a greenhouse in Iceland

Café in a hydroponic greenhouse in Iceland

1

PICKING A SYSTEM

Research is what I'm doing when I don't know what I'm doing.

— WERNHER VON BRAUN

I n this chapter, we'll talk about what hydroponics is about and why you might choose this option of gardening when there are several other methods to choose from, like container, hanging, or raised-bed gardens. Research and new discoveries have always introduced alternative ideas for how to do things into the minds of past generations, and it continues to this day. When we have the ability to improve our current conditions and make our future better, why not take that opportunity? Let's start by discussing what hydroponics is, and then we'll dig a little deeper into the details.

WHAT IS HYDROPONICS?

Hydroponics is a Latin word that means "working water." According to the Merriam-Webster dictionary, hydroponics is "the growing of plants in nutrient solutions with or without an inert medium (such as soil) to provide mechanical support" (n.d.-c). In other words, hydroponic gardening uses only water, nutrient solutions, a medium other than soil, and oxygen to grow plants. If we go back in history, we can see different forms of hydroponic gardens in use, such as when Marco Polo discovered some floating gardens in China in the 13th century. In fact, one of the seven ancient wonders of the world is hydroponics. The Hanging Gardens of Babylon were a breathtaking sight on the Euphrates River with its luxurious garden walls. Hydroponic gardening has even made more recent history when it was used on a NASA space station (Robinson, 2019). With these examples, we can see how sustainable agriculture has provided support to mankind throughout history.

In addition to being sustainable, this method is simple, easy, and cost-effective. As you learn about the process, you will begin to see how efficient and beneficial it can be for you and your family.

Lastly, there are two kinds of hydroponic systems. One is the passive system, which does not involve any equipment such as pumps to circulate air in the nutrient solution to the roots, and the other is the active system, which involves the use of pumps to help with the intake of nutrients and proper circulation.

WHY SHOULD YOU CHOOSE HYDROPONICS?

After having done my own research on this topic, I've found that there are so many advantages to hydroponic gardening. Here are several reasons you might decide to use hydroponics to grow your plants:

- You live somewhere that can reach extreme temperatures, such as the desert or high altitudes.
- You do not have access to a garden space or healthy soil.
- You'd prefer to avoid frequent use of pesticides.
- You want your crops to grow faster.
- You do not want to worry about having to maintain the quality of your soil.

If you consider the advantages as well as the properties of hydroponics, you will be able to judge for yourself how hydroponics can work for you. Here are some of the most notable properties of hydroponics:

- It can be used on nonarable land.
- Growth rates are much faster and crop yields are much higher.
- The growing medium can be reused.
- It is environmentally friendly.
- The nutrient content can be controlled.
- Temperature and pH conditions can be controlled.
- Due to control over environmental factors, hydroponics produces good, healthy vegetation.
- Pest control is simpler and the application of pesticides is not always required.

- Hydroponically grown produce is arguably better tasting than soil-grown vegetables and fruits.
- The nutrient solutions can be recycled.

As you begin implementing hydroponics in your garden, you are sure to discover these and the many other advantages of this growing method. Now, I'd like to provide some useful tips for newcomers to the hydroponics world.

THE GERMINATION OF SEEDS

In order to successfully grow your own garden, whether indoors or out, and produce a good harvest of healthy plants, you need to have a basic understanding of the life cycle of a plant or crop. Growing hydroponic plants in your own garden is only possible when you have a good starting, or seeding, process. In this section, I'll explain the germination process so you have a clear understanding of how it all begins.

In simple terms, plants grow in the following phases:

1. Sprout
2. Seedling
3. Vegetative
4. Budding
5. Flowering
6. Ripening

The Germination Process

There are many factors that can influence seed germination, which is simply the process of beginning to grow. The seed contains an embryo and a supply of food. When germination starts, the seed breaks open and the root comes out, reaching to the ground or medium looking for water, and the shoot moves upward for light. The first leaves, called "cotyledons," start to grow. Some plants grow one or two leaves at the beginning, which are called mono-cotyledons and dicotyledons, respectively. There are important environmental conditions to consider during the germination process for your hydroponic plants:

- light
- temperature
- moisture
- air

It's important to keep in mind that every kind of plant needs a different level and combination of these conditions when planting your hydroponic garden. Further, the number of hours of light a plant requires will vary at each stage of growth. It's helpful to keep a record of these times to ensure optimal growth for your plants. I'll discuss the number of hours of light needed for different kinds of plants a little later.

Germination of seeds in coco coir

Seed germination in a Rockwool medium

While your plants are in the germination stage, you must use specialized tools and resources, such as germination trays, which are available at any gardening supply store. The seeds may germinate even after placing them in the medium in your hydroponic garden, but the medium needs to be fully saturated with water. We'll go over the various kinds of mediums in more detail in Chapter 3.

TOP 5 THINGS A HYDROPONICS BEGINNER NEEDS TO KNOW

As a beginner, you may feel a bit lost at the thought of how to start a sustainable gardening practice—and how to obtain the best results. Here are some tips to help you get off to the best start possible:

- **Start small:** Starting small means you do not have to be extravagant in your preparations, like building a huge garden or planting too many plants. You are new to this, so hold some space for improving your skills and increasing your knowledge.
- **Start simple:** There are many ways you can use hydroponics, but you may want to choose the easiest and simplest method to start with. For example, you may opt for herbs and smaller plants that require only nutrients in the beginning.
- **Use good-quality supplies:** Try to avoid wasting money on products that do not support your hydroponic plant requirements or are poor in quality. It's essential to consider the best quality nutrients, pH meters, LED grow lights, and net pots for your garden. You can find everything online or at your local gardening store.
- **Don't let mistakes stop you:** You will likely make a mistake or two when you start incorporating hydroponic methods in your garden, but don't give up! Trying something new can often be difficult at first, but sooner or later you will get the hang of it. Learn from your mistakes, and try something different the next time.
- **Do your research:** If you are a beginner and have no idea how and when to start your hydroponic garden, this book is a great first resource, but you can also go online to learn even more about the topic. Use keywords such as "hydroponic gardening," "nutrients for hydroponics," and "gardening without soil" in your online searches.

WHAT DO YOU NEED TO START WITH?

If you want to start simple, look around your home for materials and resources you may already have. This will save you time and money instead of having to visit a store to get started. I recommend starting out by growing herbs and small plants like bok choy, kale, basil, or parsley.

The simplest hydroponics system you can use at home is called the deep water culture system. For this system, you only need a few items, some of which you may already have! Here are the main items you need for the deep water culture technique:

- a storage container or bucket
- an air pump with air stone
- a pH meter
- a pipette
- some net pots
- a medium such as Rockwool plug or clay pellets
- hard water liquid nutrients

The method you use for assembling your hydroponic system will depend on the materials you choose, but here are the basic steps:

1. Make sure your container is clean and opaque.
2. Make holes large enough for the pots in the lid of the container using a drill.
3. Place the medium you chose into the net pots with the seeds or sprouted seedlings.
4. Fill the container—also called the reservoir—with water and add the nutrients as directed by the packaging.

5. Connect the air pump and place the air stone in the water solution.
6. Place the pots with the medium and plant or seeds in the holes in the lid.

Once you are done setting up, you will need to do some continuous maintenance:

- Make sure the water level does not get too low, dropping no more than 1–2 inches, and that the water is always touching the plant roots.
- The pH level should be checked regularly and kept at the ideal level for your specific plants.
- Remember to keep the reservoir clean by using a bleach solution and rinsing it well. Change the water every 21 days.

There are many options and methods when it comes to hydroponics, but the best way to start is with the easiest and simplest one. You will become more skilled at hydroponic gardening as you keep learning more about it and incorporating new plants, materials, and techniques. It's important to start by choosing the system that works best with your needs and resources, such as available space and how much money you want to spend. In the next section, we'll look at various types of hydroponic systems so you can make the best decision for your needs.

HOW DO YOU CHOOSE A HYDROPONIC SYSTEM?

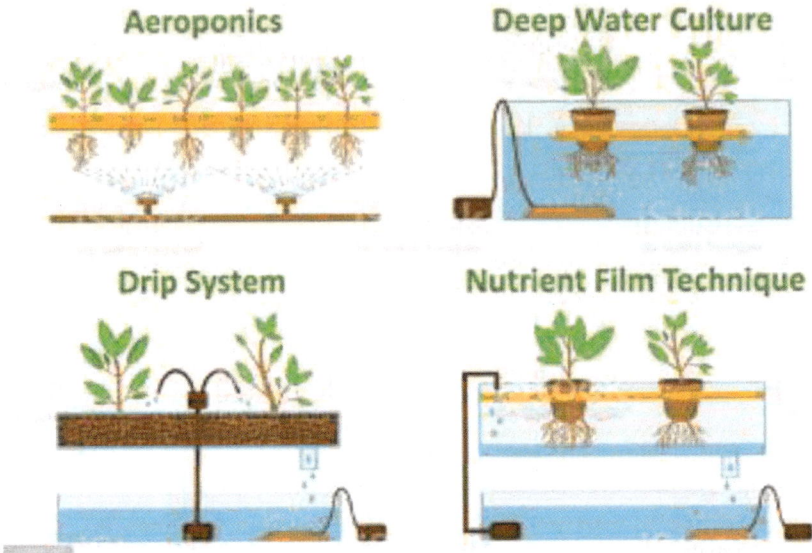

Let's recap: I've introduced what hydroponics is and how it can benefit you, and we've discussed the simplest hydroponic system for starting small as a beginner, but there are many options for hydroponic setups. Let's now take a look at some of those options and talk about how each one works.

Ebb and Flow System

Ebb and flow hydroponic system

This system works with the help of gravity and consists of a tray for your pots above a reservoir of nutrient solution and water. A pump helps fill the tray with water and allows the plants to touch the water and nutrients for a while. The water flow is stopped by turning off the pump, which causes the water level to go down—this rising and falling action is where the name "ebb and flow system" comes from. This is similar to irrigation techniques used for agricultural land but adapted for a smaller area. A timer regulates the water flow in and out of the reservoir. This cycle repeats every 45 minutes several times a day. You may even have two or three pumps that are timed to turn on and off at intervals, but this depends on the type of vegetation you are growing and its time of growth. This method allows fresh oxygen to flow to the roots, providing a good supply of oxygen to your plants. One thing to note about this system is that it's crucial to keep the pump control maintained by checking it regularly to ensure it is working properly.

Nutrient Film Technique

Nutrient film technique system

The nutrient film technique (NFT) system is considered a resource-saving technique as it uses recycled nutrients. A nutrient film is a layer of dissolved nutrients that is constantly present and being pumped throughout the system. Nutrients are continuously and efficiently supplied to your plants from a tray holding this nutrient film into which the pots containing your plants and mediums are placed. The continuous flow of liquid also ensures the presence of oxygen. Vegetables and leafy greens grow best in this hydroponic system.

Drip System

Drip system inside indoor hydroponic tent with reflective walls and LED lighting

This system is the favorite of many hydroponic gardeners. It uses water efficiently and prevents plants from drying out and becoming oversaturated with water. Water is pumped through a drip system with pipes and valves into the pots of plants to the roots and falls down into a reservoir. The nutrient solution is also pumped up from the reservoir with drips. You can dispose of the used water or recycle it and use it again. The plant roots are always aerated properly as they are not constantly soaked in water throughout the system. Drip systems can be big or small depending on the space you have available for your hydroponic garden. There are two types of drip systems: circulating and noncirculating. As the name implies, the circulating system involves the constant cycling of water and nutrients; the pH and nutrient solutions need to be checked periodically in a circulating system. The noncirculating system involves the application of water and nutrients at once, and no pump or electricity is required.

Aeroponic System

Aeroponic system with green lettuce sprouts

This system is one of a kind and involves a continuous flow of air through the plants, which can be hung, while the plant's roots are sprayed with water to keep them moist. High-pressure spraying pumps apply this mist to the plant's roots with nutrients broken down into particles. The plants are always supplied with oxygen due to this constant spray of water. It has been found that aeroponic systems can help plants grow twice as fast as other techniques (*4 Types of Hydroponics*, 2016). This is somewhat similar to the vertical system of hydroponics and has the advantage of saving space as the plants are suspended in the air. You can decorate your rooftop or terrace with a beautiful hanging garden for a natural aesthetic.

Deep Water Culture System

Deep water culture system

The deep water culture (DWC) system is considered one of the simpler options, in part because the start-up doesn't require as much effort as other methods. Also known as a water culture system, this technique has the advantage of allowing the roots of your plants to be in direct contact with the nutrient solution, and plants tend to grow faster. Another benefit of this method is that there are multiple variations gardeners can choose from. Commercially available stand-alone "tents" with reflective interior walls for LED light reflection can act as a small greenhouse. These range from $100–$200.

Wick System

Wick system setup

This system does not need the use of electricity, pumps, or aerators. The plants are placed in an absorbent medium, such as vermiculite or perlite, and nylon wicks are placed around the plants when put into the nutrient solution. The best plants to grow with this method are small herbaceous plants that need fewer nutrients to thrive. The nutrient and water content is somewhat limited in the wick system, so you may need to add some extra nutrients to the water periodically. The wick system can be used by anyone and is on the simpler side as well. If you don't have much space, this system may be a good choice for you.

Vertical System

Vertical hydroponic system

The vertical system for hydroponic gardens is a space saver when it comes to limited areas in your home or garden. The plants are arranged vertically to conserve floor space while maximizing the growing area. This system is ideal for easy maintenance and optimal light exposure. Horizontal systems may have more options when it comes to planting methods, but if you don't have the space, a vertical system may be your best bet.

Kratky Method

The Kratky method with spider plant

The Kratky method is the simplest and least expensive hydroponic gardening technique, and it is similar to the deep water culture system but without the pump. This means no electricity is required, making it even more cost-effective. In this system, only a nutrient solution, air, water, and light are needed for the plant to survive. The plant is placed in the nutrient solution with a medium —preferably hydroton—and the plant is fixed in place by a lid on top. The roots are half submerged and half exposed to air to ensure oxygen reaches the roots.

COMMON BEGINNER ERRORS

It's easy to decide on a whim to make certain changes or tweaks when trying to set up the best garden possible; however, sometimes our own ideas can unintentionally lead us astray, creating problems down the road. Here are a few common mistakes beginners make when first setting up their hydroponic garden:

- You may think fluorescent lights are a good option for two reasons: aesthetics and cost. However, the truth is that fluorescent lights are more expensive than LED lights and only provide one kind of light from the full spectrum, which is not adequate for optimal plant growth. Also, it's more expensive to maintain fluorescent lights, so you may be better off choosing something that imitates sunlight more closely and provides sufficient light.
- You may want to provide plenty of water and fertilizer to your plants, but it's critical to be aware of the quantity you are providing. You want to avoid oversaturating or overfeeding your plants, and using too much fertilizer may cause unwanted deposition of salts and the growth of fungus.
- Try to use materials and supplies recommended for hydroponics. There are endless options for gardening tools and supplies, but those specific to hydroponic gardening will give you the best outcomes. For example, there are certain fertilizers that are more effective than others when used in a hydroponic garden.
- Sometimes understanding the pH level of a nutrient solution can be tricky, but a pH that is too low can be detrimental to the overall nutrient content. To avoid this, you want to maintain an optimum pH for your

hydroponics system—around 5.5–6.5 on the acidity scale (Courtney, 2019b). The pH levels vary for many reasons in a hydroponic system, so it's important to know the right pH for your type of plant.

Picking the system that's right for you will require some work on your part, but the results are worth the time and energy spent on making your decision. Once you've done that, the next step in creating your hydroponic garden is determining where and how big you want it to be, which we will discuss in the next chapter.

2

SIZE AND PLACEMENT

Productivity is never an accident. It is always the result of a commitment to excellence, intelligent planning, and focused effort.

— PAUL J. MEYER

Gardeners like us have so many options for how to install and display a productive hydroponic garden in our homes, lawns, open spaces, or enclosed rooms. It all depends on the size and kind of plants you want to grow. Small plants and herbs require minimal feeding and space to grow efficiently, but bigger plants like fruits and flowers require a little more of both. Different plants also have different sunlight and air needs throughout each of their growth stages. In this chapter, I will be discussing the various factors you'll need to consider as you determine the size and placement of your hydroponic system so you can decide how to best plant your garden with the space and resources available to you.

Ultimately, you want to choose a location for your hydroponic garden that will provide optimal light—whether from the sun or artificial—as well as make it easy to deliver proper water and nutrients to your plants. The equipment you need can be purchased or made by you.

WHERE IS THE BEST SPOT TO PUT YOUR HYDROPONIC SYSTEM?

Hydroponic gardens can go indoors or out and are a great option when you have limited space. While looking for a place to install your garden, keep the following in mind:

- They need 4–6 hours of sunlight each day.
- Indoor gardens will require grow lights.
- Ideal temperatures for your plants to grow need to be provided and maintained, usually around 65–80 °F (18–27 °C).
- Because some hydroponic systems require electricity, you'll need to set it up so that the electrical elements won't get wet or take steps to ensure they won't be damaged when it rains or snows.
- Make sure to set your system up close to a reliable power source.
- Your system should have an easily accessible water source nearby.

When you cannot provide the required sunlight for your plants, you may have to install a high-intensity discharge (HID) lamp that will supply sufficient light for your garden. Another choice is Gro-Lites, which are available at gardening stores. These fluorescent lights are good for planting wandering Jew or similar plants that do not need much sunlight. For vegetables like tomatoes and beans, you'll have to provide maximum light during the day.

HOW BIG CAN YOU GO WITH YOUR HYDROPONICS SYSTEM?

The greatest thing about hydroponics is that you can place it anywhere you want—on a wall, in a 3D box, or even suspended in the air. Therefore, space can be a flexible factor when installing your hydroponic garden. Your hydroponic garden can grow in as small a space as 12 x 24 x 60 in. (30.5 x 61 x 152 cm) (Adriana, 2023). The possible locations for hydroponic gardens range from basements all the way up to large greenhouses, so size is not a limiting factor. The main difference is you need extra lighting and possibly a heat source for enclosed or cold areas such as basements or closets. A greenhouse is the most efficient way to grow fruits and vegetables. Next, we'll take a closer look at indoor, outdoor, and limited-space hydroponic gardens as well as greenhouses.

Indoor Hydroponic Garden

Indoor hydroponic gardening can be very exciting. If you are setting up your hydroponic garden inside, make sure it is situated near a window or any place in your home with a good source of sunlight. You may still need to set up some appliances, such as an electric pump, to keep your garden working, so choose a spot for your garden where it will be easy to get water and power to it. All you need is a support structure, a growing medium, seedlings or starter plants, good nutrients, and light.

Outdoor Hydroponic Garden

Outdoor hydroponic gardens are one of the most efficient options as they have access to the best source of sunlight, nutrients, oxygen, and water from rain or irrigation systems. Plants may grow faster in outdoor environments, and you can lower your expenses for lighting purposes as you have an unlimited supply of natural light. Make sure to keep a tank of cool water in your hydroponic system since the temperature may rise outdoors on some days, which could lead to plants using more moisture than usual. Another thing to consider outdoors is the amount of air available. Of course, it is very good for plants to get a good supply of fresh air, but you might need to protect the plants from strong winds. Too much aeration in plant leaves can have an adverse effect on growth. Another issue to be aware of with an outdoor setup is pests. One method to counteract potential pest problems is to plant specific vegetation surrounding the hydroponic plants. For example, if you are growing plants that are susceptible to aphids or spider mites, which are pests that damage plants, you could add vegetation that will cover your hydroponic plants, essentially creating a shield to protect them.

Limited-Space Hydroponic Garden

This kind of hydroponic setup might go in a closet, a small nook, or even the basement; small herbs and medicinal plants can do well in these types of spaces. If your limited space is indoors, you can use walls, windowsills, or any flat surface near a light source. If your indoor space is a closet or basement, be sure to think about how you will supply light and water to your plants. Since there is often no sunlight available in these spaces, the only way to provide adequate light to your plants is with a lighting system, and you may have to add a small-area space heater. For your basement, you may find a spot that receives some sunlight if there is a window, but make sure it will be able to provide light for up to six hours a day. Outdoors, you can put your hydroponic system anywhere on your patio or deck, lawn, garden, or greenhouse.

Hydroponic Greenhouses

A hydroponic greenhouse is an excellent—though much more involved—way to start your hydroponic garden. An outdoor greenhouse with enough space and light where you can control the temperature and humidity is arguably every gardener's ultimate dream. Vegetables are often easily grown in a greenhouse, and you can grow tomatoes, cucumbers, or melons even during the coldest winters. To set up a greenhouse, there are certain factors you need to consider, such as the following:

- Place your greenhouse in a location that gets sufficient sunlight.
- Place it near your home to provide easier access to power and water supplies.
- Ensure proper ventilation for good airflow.
- You can use wet cloths, fans, or other cooling methods if your greenhouse becomes too warm for your plants.

THINGS TO CONSIDER

You may have a list of your favorite plants you want to grow in your hydroponic garden, and you know vegetables and herbs can be grown year-round, but there are some factors to consider before you get started that will help you avoid problems down the road. A few of these are

- light source
- water source
- humid atmosphere
- protection from strong wind
- supply of nutrients
- suitable growth medium
- good support system

The cost of greenhouses can vary and depends on what you can afford to spend. If you want to build a greenhouse with real glass, it may cost thousands of dollars but last many years. Otherwise, you may opt for a do-it-yourself (DIY) greenhouse that you can build yourself. You can find tips and how-tos on YouTube or look into buying a simple greenhouse kit, which are readily available at gardening and home improvement stores.

With good maintenance and resources, you can feed a family of four with just a few square feet. If you have a larger area, you may be able to grow enough food to sell at a farmers market or even set up a commercial supply chain if your operation is big enough.

As you consider everything discussed in this chapter, it's important to have a good foundation when starting your hydroponic system, which we will talk more about in the next chapter!

GOOD FOUNDATIONS

— JAMES CASH PENNEY

I n order to have a strong foundation for your hydroponic garden, you need to give special attention to the materials you use and their quality first. When planting hydroponically, your medium or substrate should be of the best quality. There are several choices when it comes to mediums; a substrate is a mixture of multiple elements, such as perlite, peat moss, or vermiculite without soil, and a medium is usually just one element or ingredient, such as coco coir. Thus, the foundation of your hydroponic garden is essentially what you decide to plant your plants in.

Here are some basic first steps for setting up your hydroponic garden:

1. Soak the medium or substrate in water for at least 24 hours to remove any dirt or matter that might affect the pH.
2. Place your net pots in fresh water in your container or reservoir. You'll want net pots made of high-quality plastic with slits at the bottom; these can be found at any gardening store and come in various sizes.
3. Place the medium or substrate into the net pots.

You can reuse the substrate, but only after cleaning and sanitizing it to avoid pathogens.

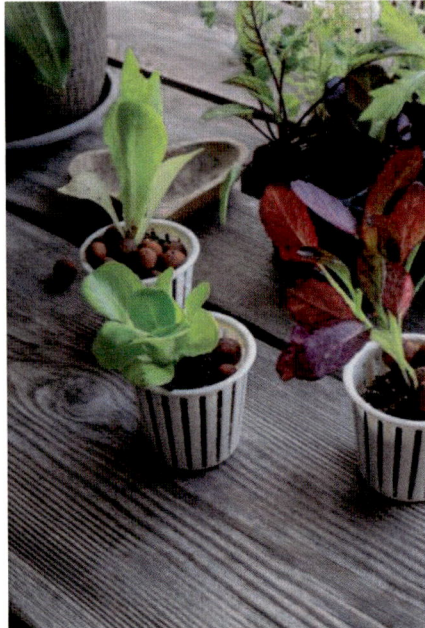

Net pots

HOW TO CHOOSE A GROWING MEDIUM

The medium used in a hydroponic garden can affect the nutrient level, pH, and moisture content of the whole system. The medium should be able to hold moisture and keep the pH level steady. Often, the medium may contain minerals that could improve your plant's growth. Therefore, choosing the right medium is essential to ensure it is beneficial to your plant rather than harmful. There are a wide variety of options for mediums and substrates, but here are some of the more common ones:

- Rockwool
- perlite
- vermiculite
- coco substrate
- LECA
- clay pebbles

Some of these are more suited to indoor setups versus outdoor, some are better for organic gardening, and some are more compatible with certain kinds of hydroponic systems. In this section, we'll look at various types of mediums and substrates and the pros and cons of each.

Rockwool

Rockwool is a material similar to wool made by blowing steam through melted rock.

+ Pros

- Comes in many shapes and sizes
- Pores provide space for root growth
- Restores oxygen levels
- High water absorption capacity

— Cons

- Not biodegradable
- May affect pH due to its alkalinity

Perlite

Perlite is an ore that is heated to expand into an absorbent puff.

+ Pros

- Can take any shape
- Restores oxygen levels
- Cost-effective

— Cons

- Nonrenewable
- Has a tendency to attach to small particles that could cause the growth of algae

Vermiculite

Vermiculite is a mineral ore made of hydrous phyllosilicate.

+ Pros

- Has an almost neutral pH
- Good water retention
- Holds in nutrients

− Cons

- Uses more moisture
- Nonrenewable

Coco Coir

Coco coir is a coconut husk by-product.

+ Pros

- Good water retention
- Organic material

− Cons

- Forms like a brick and dries out quickly
- Changes form

Pumice

Pumice is volcanic rock with pores.

+ Pros

- Many available sizes
- Bigger ones allow more air to pass through

- Lightweight

— **Cons**

- May vary in quality
- May be too lightweight for some uses

Hydroton

Hydroton, also known as light expanded clay aggregate (LECA), is clay pebbles that have been stretched or expanded to the size of marbles.

+ **Pros**

- Lightweight
- Provides a space for airflow and root growth
- Can be reused
- Easy to clean

— **Cons**

- Holds water for a limited time
- Expensive

Gravel

Gravel is fairly common and is small rocks that can come from many sources.

+ Pros

- Cost-effective
- Easy to clean and use

— Cons

- Can collect algae
- Affects the pH
- Heavy weight

Lights, growing mediums, and germination supplies from a hydroponic supply store

Coco coir

WHAT ARE THE BEST SUPPLEMENTS?

Plants require certain nutrients that are vital for their growth. There are around 17 important nutrients plants need, and they can be grouped as micronutrients and macronutrients. Micronutrients are needed in smaller amounts than macronutrients, but your plants will need sufficient amounts of each, and they will be delivered to your plants through the atmosphere and the nutrient solution and medium you use. In this section, we'll discuss each of these nutrients and how they help support your plants' growth.

Macronutrients

- hydrogen
- oxygen

- nitrogen
- carbon
- phosphorus
- potassium
- calcium
- magnesium
- sulfur

Micronutrients

- manganese
- boron
- zinc
- chlorine
- copper
- nickel
- iron
- molybdenum

Supply of micronutrients at a wholesale store

In the tables below, you'll see each nutrient, its importance and composition, and how it provides nutrition for plants (Sanchez et al., 2023).

Macronutrients

Supplement	Percentage (%)	Role	Source
Calcium (Ca)	1.5	• Activates enzymes • Helps preserve cell structure	Calcium or Ca^{2+}
Potassium (K)	2	• Activates enzymes • Helps improve turgor pressure in plant cells and keeps them hydrated • Regulates osmosis	Potassium or K^+
Magnesium (Mg)	0.4	• Activates enzymes • Acts as a component of chlorophyll	Magnesium or Mg^{2+}
Phosphorus (P)	0.4	• Supports metabolism as ATP or NADP (di- and triphosphates) • Exists as phospholipids in membranes	Hydrogen phosphate $(H2PO4^-)$ and dihydrogen phosphate $(HPO4^{2+})$
Sulfur (S)	0.5	• Present in nucleic acids • Exists as a component of amino acids and proteins and as coenzyme A	Sulfate $(SO4^-)$
Nitrogen (N)	2–4	• Exists as a component of amino acids • Acts as a coenzyme • Present in nucleic acids	Nitrate (NO_3^-) and ammonium $(NH4^+)$
Carbon (C), hydrogen (H), and oxygen (O)	90+	• Present as components of organic compounds	Carbon dioxide (CO_2) and water (H_2O)

Micronutrients

Supplement	Percentage (%)	Role	Source
Manganese (Mn)	0.02	• Activates enzymes • Participates in splitting water	Manganese (Mn^{2+})
Iron (Fe)	0.02	• Participates in redox (oxidation and reduction reactions) changes • Helps in photosynthesis • Helps in respiration	Iron (Fe^{2+})
Molybdenum (Mo)	Negligible	• Participates in redox changes • Helps nitrate reduction	Molybdate (MoO_4^{2-})
Copper (Cu)	Negligible	• Participates in redox changes • Helps in photosynthesis • Helps in respiration	Copper (Cu^{2+})
Nickel (Ni)	0.000005–0.0005	• Exists as a component of some enzymes • Maintains biological nitrogen fixation • Helps in nitrogen metabolism	Nickel (Ni^{2+})
Chlorine (Cl)	0.1–2	• Keeps a balance in ionic charge • Participates in splitting water	Chlorine (Cl^-)
Boron (B)	0.01	• Participates in membrane activity • Helps in cell division	Borate (B^{3-})
Zinc (Zn)	Negligible	• Participates as an enzyme cofactor activator	Zinc (Zn^{2+})

Hydroponic nutrients

HOW DO YOU MONITOR AND MEASURE THE GROWING MEDIUM AND NUTRIENTS?

Hydroponics is a unique process of growing plants if you have a good environment and foundation. The foundation for a hydroponic system is the medium and nutrient solution you use to plant your seedlings at the very beginning. Now you have a good basic understanding of the importance of components such as pH, temperature, air quality, and moisture content for your hydroponic garden. You also know that you need to regulate and monitor the nutrients being used in the entire system and that the pH of the nutrient solution should generally be somewhere between 5.5 and 6.5. You can find a pH meter online or at a gardening store.

When there is a big difference in the levels of concentration of minerals between the plant and the nutrient solution, osmosis may occur. When this happens, something called fertilizer burn can happen, which results in wilting or browning of your plant (Chartier, 2021). This will affect its growth, and every plant species has a specific tolerance level for acidity and alkalinity. To avoid this, you need to know whether there are excess salts present in the water. This measurement will also tell if your nutrient solution is acidic or alkaline.

Electrical conductivity, total dissolved solids, and dissolved oxygen are the three parameters that can help you measure the nutrient levels in your hydroponic garden. You need to monitor and keep a record of these to keep growing your plants in the most favorable conditions. Let's look at each of these in more detail so you can effectively monitor these parameters in your hydroponic garden.

1. **Electrical conductivity (EC):** Electrical conductivity is a measure of ions present in the water solution because ions in a liquid or substance will conduct electricity. In the case of hydroponics, the ions we are concerned with are salts such as calcium, phosphate, sulfates, and nitrates. The electrical conductivity will show a high concentration when there is a high amount of these salt ions. This can be measured by connecting an ion meter to your hydroponic system. An ion meter consists of two-pole electrodes or sensors—or both—that are used to detect the electrical conductivity, or the ion concentration, of the water solution. This ion concentration will help predict the amount of electrical conductivity because it is proportional to this concentration.

2. **Total dissolved solids (TDS):** Total dissolved solids can indicate whether dissolved salts are present in the nutrient solution as well as the amount of salts present, giving you valuable information before you add any supplements. The TDS measurement indicates the salt concentration and thus the conductivity.

3. **Dissolved oxygen (DO):** Oxygen is an essential component for plants, and dissolved oxygen helps plant respiration. When the dissolved oxygen level is low, it means there are impurities present in the water. If the DO is at the optimum level—5 mg/L—then the water is suitable for planting. Without this level, it will be difficult to grow your crops safely and healthily. This is a newer concept for many hydroponic gardeners and farmers.

These parameters are all important to track and record as you move forward with hydroponic gardening. If you have good control over these parameters, your plants will thrive. To find instruments to measure all of these parameters, you can search online or visit your nearest gardening or aquaculture store.

The table below shows the growth stages of plants from young to fruit and their nutrient requirements. Plants need different amounts of every nutrient at each stage of their growth. Newly transplanted plants also require particular nutrients.

Growth stage	Essential nutrients
Young plant stage	Nitrogen and traces of all nutrients
Vegetative stage	Nitrogen
Blossoming stage	Phosphorus, potassium, and calcium
Fruiting stage	Phosphorus, potassium, and nitrogen (trace amounts)
Newly transplanted	Phosphorus and potassium

When you have created a good foundation, you will be on your way to having a healthy hydroponic garden. It does require some time and effort, but having a sustainable hydroponic gardening system is worth it.

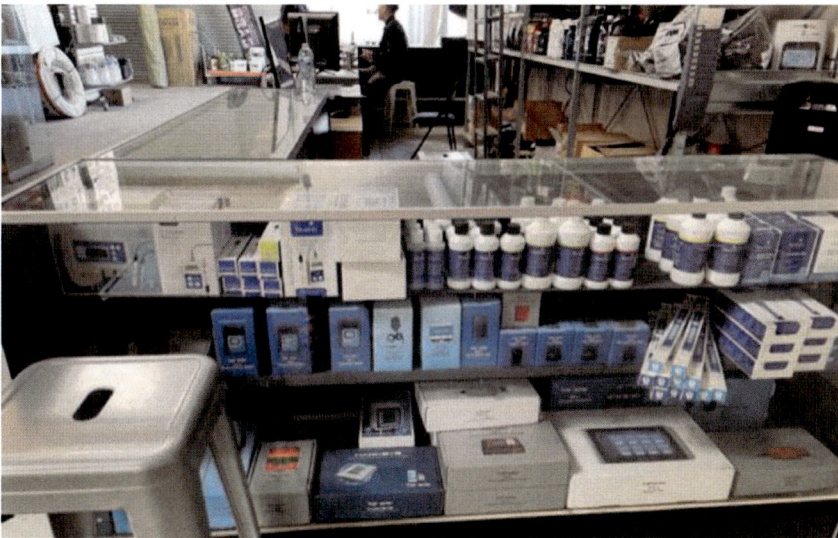

Testing supplies for hydroponic gardens

4

HEALTHY, HAPPY HYDROPONICS

Expect problems and eat them for breakfast.

— ALFRED A. MONTAPERT

O nce you have all the resources and equipment prepared for your hydroponic garden, you want to start thinking about how you will maintain the health of your plants by considering how you'll deal with challenges such as diseases and pests. Indoor hydroponics may face problems with diseases that occur in warm, humid environments, so this chapter will talk about some of these and how you can avoid them. Once you get an idea of how to best manage pests and diseases, you can run your garden with no interruptions all year.

MILDEW AND MOLD

The most common mold that occurs are fungi that grow on your plant's leaves. You can simply remove the affected leaves or stems from the plant to keep it from spreading. It's important to catch these types of mold as early as possible to minimize the harm they can do to your plant.

Mildew is a similar fungal disease that looks like a gray powder. It may not look especially harmful, but it's imperative to address it as early as possible so it doesn't spread to other plants. Mildew can be mitigated by using fungicides or removing the leaves that have been infected. You can also use a cloth to remove it at an earlier stage. Here are some tips for preventing mildew from forming in the first place:

- Wash your hands and wear gardening-specific clothing and gloves when working in your hydroponic garden to avoid bringing in outside contaminants.
- Keep the humidity lower than 50%.
- Ensure adequate air circulation indoors.
- Watch out for any dead organic materials such as plant leaves or stems.
- Clean and sanitize all your gardening equipment.

ROOT ROT

Root rot is another potential problem hydroponic gardeners might face, and it can be hard to spot through the medium. If you can see it, you should be able to identify it, but if you can't see the roots of your hydroponic plants, you'll be able to tell by the smell produced when roots start to rot. It's a sulfuric smell like rotten eggs or flowers left in a vase for too long. Root rot also causes a decrease in pH. You can monitor the pH by periodically testing it using a simple pH testing kit. It's important to address this issue before your plants start to wilt. Here are some things you can do to prevent root rot:

- Be sure to wash your hands and wear your dedicated gardening gear.
- Clean and sanitize all equipment used in your garden.
- Use dark or opaque containers to prevent the growth of algae in your plant's surroundings.
- Allow for air circulation before you water your medium.
- Take measures to keep pests from entering the environment.
- Try to keep the nutrient solution temperature below 75 °F (24 °C).

COMMON PESTS

Pests can be a problem, especially for outdoor hydroponic gardens. Indoor gardens are more controlled, making it easier to avoid pests. Some of the most common pests you may face are spider mites, aphids, whiteflies, and thrips. Here are the kinds of damage these critters may cause to your plants:

- **Greenhouse whitefly (Trialeurodes vaporariorum):** Whiteflies pierce plants with their mouths, causing damage, and they leave behind a residue of honeydew, which turns into a mold.
- **Two-spotted spider mites (Tetranychus urticae):** Also known as red spider mites, these pests can cause damage such as interveinal chlorosis, stunted growth, and leaf

diseases to your plants. They feed on the leaves and stems of their host plant.

- **Aphids (any species):** Aphids are harmful to plants and leave a deposit of honeydew. They also cause the growth of mold, which can spread to the entire plant over time. Aphids inhibit the growth of new foliage and leave a sooty residue. Spraying the foliage with isopropyl alcohol can be effective against aphids and won't damage the plant.
- **Western flower thrips (Frankliniella occidentalis):** Flower thrips can hide in budding flowers and leaves of a plant and may damage it by distorting the growth of new leaves and foliage. They can also be carriers of tomato spotted wilt virus, so it's important to be diligent about avoiding them.

If you have problems identifying a potential pest in your hydroponic garden, collect a sample in a clear jar and take it to be evaluated. If you know a master gardener in your area, they would be a good resource, or you can check with employees at a local gardening center.

HOW TO HEAD OFF PROBLEMS

There are many ways you can prevent pests and diseases to protect your plants. You may be worried that it will take a lot of time and money, but there are many efficient and cost-effective options available. If you proactively create a prevention strategy, you can be free from the nuisance of pest invasions. Here are some tips to keep those critters out of your hydroponic garden:

- Inspect and clean every plant you add to your garden.
- Place a few insect repelling or trapping devices, such as sticky cards, around the garden area.
- Wear your dedicated gardening clothes or cover your clothing with a lab coat or other outer layer when working in your garden.
- Sanitize your greenhouse and garden equipment before or during assembly. One good way to do this is by washing your equipment with bleach water and rinsing thoroughly.
- Get rid of any debris lying around your greenhouse to avoid any pests settling there, such as on benches or the ground.
- Inspect your plants daily and check for signs of pests that may be present under the leaves, between branches, and in the roots.
- Barriers like nets can help prevent insects from reaching your plants.
- Try arranging your plants according to their species and susceptibility to pests.

FIXING AND CONTROLLING PROBLEMS

If you do discover pests in your garden, you can seek help from growth regulators, biological remedies, and safe pesticides. All three can help you control and manage your unwanted guests. Pest management is a process, and researchers have presented a number of new ideas. For organic gardens, there are options such as semiochemicals (behavior-modifying compounds), organic pesticides, and botanical biopesticides (Weintraub et al., 2017).

To control your hydroponic garden pests and diseases, you can implement the following techniques:

Phytosanitation: Phytosanitation is a process used internationally to avoid the transportation of pests and plant diseases across borders without following guidelines and regulations for sanitation. This system was introduced for the purpose of regulating the trade of ornamental plants in the United States (Weintraub et al., 2017). In the case of organic agricultural crops or greenhouse gardens, the same concept can be applied. Basically, you have to do the following:

1. Disinfect the pathways into the greenhouse or garden area to lower the chances of pathogens entering.
2. Disinfect the surroundings of your hydroponic garden and places that are susceptible to infection.
3. Install a sanitation station with water, soap, and sanitizer for cleaning yourself and all the items you bring into your garden.
4. Dispose of any infected or dead plants to avoid the spread of pathogens.
5. Avoid any stray water droplets or condensation that may create a possibility of growing pathogens in and around the greenhouse.

Controlling growing medium: When choosing a medium, be careful to look for one that is organically certified and does not attract pests or develop diseases.

Solarization: This method involves trapping solar energy by placing a plastic cover over your plants in order to try and inhibit the growth or living conditions for pathogens or pests.

Solarization kills eggs and larvae of pests and thus prevents their existence in your plants.

Biological control: This method uses one organism as a biological control agent (BCA) to get rid of another. The BCA will feed on or kill pathogens or bacteria, eliminating them from your plant. Predators, parasitoids, or entomopathogens are commonly used as biological control agents.

Secondary plants: Secondary plants can be used as a bank or breeding ground for pests that can be useful to another plant. For example, in the United Kingdom, banker plants were home to a number of parasitoids that soon controlled the spread of aphids in fruits and vegetables. Non-crop and insectary plants can act as banks where parasitoids that are helpful to your garden can live.

Semiochemicals: Semiochemicals are chemicals produced by smaller organisms, such as pathogens, and send signals to insects or pests to attract or get rid of them, so semiochemicals can be used as attractants or repellants depending on the need. Semiochemicals can also be used to disrupt any pests or insects from mating and breeding within your garden area. Often, traps such as Venus flytraps can be used to capture these critters.

Biopesticides: Biopesticides are pesticides that can be made from different organisms such as microbes; they can be plant-based or they can be a product of fermentation. They contain non-synthetic materials and have no added ingredients.

Though diseases and pests can be a nuisance in your hydroponic garden, there are ways to prevent them from getting there in the first place and ways to deal with them if they do make their way in. In the next chapter, we'll explore some important factors you'll want to consider while growing your fruits and vegetables, such as the amount, type, and intensity of sunlight your plants need.

5

FIRE AND EARTH

> *The sun is the most important thing in everybody's life, whether you're a plant, an animal or a fish, and we take it for granted.*
>
> — DANNY BOYLE

Sunlight is necessary for both humans and plants. The sun provides us with vitamins, and we have to allow sunlight, or ultraviolet (UV) light, into our gardens so they can flourish as well. Without sunlight, photosynthesis is not possible. There are particular kinds of electromagnetic waves and temperature ranges that are required for gardening and helping plants produce sufficient food. Lighting has an important part to play in indoor hydroponic gardening, and I'll get into more detail about this in this chapter.

TEMPERATURE AND ULTRAVIOLET LIGHTS FOR PLANTS

We get both visible light and infrared rays from the sun, and the spectrum of light consists of different wavelengths, or intensities, of light that cause trees and plants outdoors to grow. The sunlight, or UV light, varies from season to season, which is why it's important to know when your plants are unable to receive enough light to support their food production. The sun radiates temperatures of 5,000 Kelvin, and this range of temperature is required by plants in order to grow and produce food sufficiently, so an indoor garden needs similar conditions (MacDonald, 2017).

In order to bring this life-giving light inside, red and blue light-emitting diode (LED) lights were commonly used for indoor gardens, but white LEDs have become more popular recently as they serve the needs of the plants. White LED lights can emit temperatures of 2,700–5,000 Kelvin.

The color and temperature of light can vary, and different plants need a particular temperature or color. You will need to install the lights in your hydroponic garden according to your plants' requirements. For example, lettuce needs less sunlight compared to fruits such as strawberries or even tomatoes. This is why fruits grow much better during summer. Cauliflower and cabbages need only 12 hours of sunlight and are good vegetables to grow during fall (Johnson, 2018a).

Whether fruit, vegetable, or herb, you'll want to use your grow lights based on the needs of each plant. The table below shows the different colors and wavelengths that are ideal for different plants.

Color	Wavelength (in nanometers)	Plant	Description
Red	620–780 nm	Flowers, fruits	Helps keep plants warm and supports the growth of the stem
Green	490–570 nm	General	Can be used for any plant; usually combined with other colors
Blue	440–490 nm	Vegetables, herbs	Stimulates plant growth and development
Yellow	570–585 nm	Flowers, fruits	Helps promote plant growth in winter months
Orange	585–620 nm	Flowers, fruits	Supports plant appetite and food intake

HOW TO MANAGE LIGHT FOR YOUR HYDROPONICS

The plants in your hydroponic garden will need both direct and indirect light. Different plants will have different requirements for the number of hours of sunlight they need. Sometimes plants need a break from too much sunlight because this can affect their growth. Often, leaving your plants in direct sunlight on a hot day for too long can dry them out. Managing your lighting system properly is essential if your goal is to provide the same amount of light to your indoor plants as they would receive outdoors.

Vegetables grown outside need sunlight for 8 hours at a time. When you are using artificial lights indoors for your hydroponic system, there should be light available for at least 14–16 hours. For perennials, you may need to vary the lengths of time they are exposed to light based on where they are in their life cycle.

Some plants need shorter periods of daylight than others. This depends on when they flower as too much sunlight may disrupt that process.

The daylight cycle is shown in the table below.

Daylight	Hours of sunlight per day	Plant
Short	5–6	Herbs
Medium	12	Cauliflower, poinsettias, chrysanthemums, strawberries
Medium	14	Eggplant, roses, corn, rice
Long	18	Spinach, potatoes, turnips

In the next table, you'll find different types of lighting and plants that do best with each type.

Type of lighting	Plants & growth stages
T5 high-output fluorescent bulbs	Flowering, blooming, and growing stages
T12 fluorescent bulbs	Seeds, seedlings, and cuttings
T5 fluorescent bulbs or lamps	Small plants
HID—metal halide	Leafy or bushy plants such as lettuce, greens, herbs/growing stage
HID—high-pressure sodium	Annual flowering stage such as tomatoes or fruits/vegetative or blooming stage
LED grow lights	For large plantations and indoor gardens

There are numerous options when it comes to lighting systems today, and as we touched on earlier, the use of lighting for agriculture as well as aquaculture has risen to a commercial level. Here are some of the lighting options available to you:

- **Fluorescent bulbs:** Fluorescent bulbs, such as T12 bulbs, allow limited heat and are good for growing seeds or seedlings. This type of light is suitable for the growth of leafy greens and flowers.
- **Light-emitting diodes (LEDs):** LEDs are an efficient and cost-effective lighting option that is becoming increasingly popular among hydroponic gardeners. You can get them in the form of bulbs, tubes, or panels. Just like fluorescent bulbs, they give a nice look too.
- **High-pressure sodium bulbs (HPS):** HPS bulbs are a kind of high-intensity discharge (HID) bulb. They are slightly expensive but efficient during the fruit and flowering stages. They need to be changed every two years.
- **Metal-halide bulbs (MH):** MH bulbs are HID bulbs that cast a broad area of light and are great for long-daylight plants with their abundant bright light. This lighting system is best when plants are in the growing and vegetation stages.

Grow lights, LEDs, and others are available online and in gardening stores. Here are some bulbs I recommend:

- GE BR30 LED Grow light
- Aceple LED Grow light
- AeroGarden Bounty Basic IndoorAeroGarden Bounty Basic—Indoor Garden with LED Grow Light, Black Gardening

You can combine your lighting options, such as using both HPS and MH bulbs, to provide your plants all the types of light they need as they go through each growth stage. Lighting in your hydroponic garden can be functional and add an aesthetically pleasing touch.

HOW TO MANAGE TEMPERATURE AND HUMIDITY

You want to manage the temperature for your plants intentionally and systematically. The temperature and lighting needs for plants vary, as discussed earlier, depending on the type of plant and each stage of growth; there should be a particular temperature for the seedling, flowering, and fruit-growing stages. Similarly, the humidity levels in your garden should be maintained as the plants go through their different stages. Here are some helpful tips:

- Temperatures should be around 68–77 °F (20–25 °C) while the seedlings are growing and the lights are on.
- When the lights are off, the temperature should be between 63–68 °F (17–20 °C) to help the plant maintain a constant temperature.
- Humidity should be reduced as the seedlings mature by around 40%.
- Ensure proper ventilation to reduce the humidity by using fans, air coolers, evaporative coolers, or air conditioners.
- The humidity should be around 60–70% when the plant starts to grow.
- Keep gradually reducing the humidity as the plant goes from seedling to flowering from around 70% to 40%.

Fan supplies for hydroponic gardens in gardening store

There are a number of guidelines that can help you find the best balance of temperature and humidity for your hydroponic garden. Below are some steps you can take to help get you there.

1. Find a secure place for your hydroponic garden to grow where it won't be disturbed.
2. Look for a controlled environment that is favorable to your plants.
3. Ensure plenty of proper ventilation is in place.
4. Keep your plants' spacing uniform; a good rule of thumb is to provide one square foot, or 144 in^2 (366 cm^2), for each plant.
5. Think about insulation and how you will control air circulation. Be on the lookout for any holes or leaks that might affect air circulation. Proper insulation will also

help control the heat, temperature, and humidity in your garden.

6. It's important to be able to calculate the amount of light you want to allow in the garden area, or your "hydro room," as hydroponic gardeners call it. The amount of light that covers a certain area is measured in what is called "watts per square foot," and in this case, your target will be 50–75 watts per square foot. So for example, if your room is 180 square feet, you would multiply this by the range mentioned. For example, 50 watts per square foot: 180 x 50 = 9000 W/sq. ft. Simple math!

7. Check the power or voltage that your electricity allows you to use for the lighting system installed. Take safety precautions before connecting any electrical devices.

8. Make sure your hydro room is safe for simultaneous water and electricity use and avoid any risks.

9. Fix the temperature and humidity according to your plants' requirements. We talked earlier about how to control the heat and air circulation through ventilation. This can be done by keeping the windows open.

10. If you are using devices like dehumidifiers, high-pressure bulbs, or other heat-producing instruments, you will need to think about how you will maintain the temperature.

Some vegetables and fruits cannot withstand as much sunlight as others, and there are certain limits to be maintained in your garden. In the next chapter, we'll talk about hydroponic gardening strategies specific to growing vegetables and greens that can be used for salads.

EMPOWER OTHERS TO GROW THEIR VERY OWN HYDROPONIC GARDEN FROM SCRATCH

"The first supermarket supposedly appeared on the American landscape in 1946... Until then, where was all the food? The food was in homes, gardens, local fields, and forests. It was near kitchens, near tables, near bedsides. It was in the pantry, the cellar, the backyard."

— JOE SALATIN

Earlier in the introduction, I mentioned that people across the globe are seeking to take a more active role in producing the food they eat. We are living an authentic green revolution in which 67% of the population is growing or planning to grow edible plants, and many more are content to give life to vibrant flowers, herbs, and ornamental plants.

Today, the aim isn't simply to garden but rather to do so sustainably, with a keen awareness of preserving precious resources such as land, water, and energy. It's as though humanity has heeded to a wake-up call. Key global events and the ever-growing problem of global warming have made us snap out of our inertia and search for better solutions. And many are amazed to finally discover they no longer need to seek out food sources passively. That they have a big say in what they consume and that it is possible to tuck into delicious, fresh, pesticide-free produce grown in their one home.

By this stage in your reading, you have seen how many obstacles to leading a greener life—including a lack of space, worries about water scarcity, and time concerns—are easy to overcome through hydroponics. If you have already launched your hydroponic garden and are delighted by how easy, cheap, and quick it is to grow a myriad of plants, I hope you can share your opinion with others.

By leaving a review of this book on Amazon, you'll empower other readers to grow a bustling, colorful, resilient garden— without needing a gardening course and breaking the bank.

Simply by letting them know how this book helped you, you'll let them see that even absolute beginners can easily master the essence of hydroponics.

Thank you for your support. Your words matter. They could change someone's life and give them the gift of health—and it's all thanks to the power of gardening.

6

LEAFY GREENS AND VEGETABLES

> *My dishes tend to have a very carefree style: what's ripe at the farmers market or what's in my fridge, even if I'm cleaning out my fridge. It tends to be a very improvisational style. I major in salads, but a loose definition of salad; it can have a real robust skirt steak on top of it off the grill or quinoa or buckwheat or sprouted almond.*
>
> — DARBY STANCHFIELD

Vegetables and leafy greens are some of the most common products of gardeners, including hydroponic gardeners. The fresh, succulent taste of hydroponic vegetables has made them popular among those who have limited space or availability of sunlight. Vegetables are a staple in our everyday diets, and without them, our meals feel incomplete and our diets certainly are. Our body needs vitamins A and B and essential minerals that are all found in vegetables. Leafy greens are sources of vitamin K, which protects our body from building up too much calcium. Leafy greens and vegetables also aid in digestion and help keep us hydrated. Growing vegetables hydroponically is the cleanest, most efficient way to add greens to your daily diet, although there are some different strategies involved since you are using water and nutrient solutions to grow your vegetables rather than traditional methods using soil. Many hydroponic gardeners have great success growing vegetables, and there are a few tricks and tips you can follow to find success as well.

BEST LEAFY GREENS

Leafy greens are part of the American diet and have been for ages. Some leafy greens originated from China, Asia Minor, and the Eastern Mediterranean. Some of the more common leafy greens we love to add to our salads are spinach, kale, lettuce, and Swiss chard. Kale is a great addition to smoothies, and spinach and Swiss chard are excellent sources of vitamins and can be cooked as a part of many delicious dishes. All these leafy greens can be grown hydroponically at a low cost. Let's look at some popular leafy greens:

Spinach: Spinach is sensitive to hot climates and needs to grow in cooler temperatures around 40–70 °F (4–21 °C) Fortunately, with hydroponic gardening, this is possible. Spinach has a tendency to grow pathogens such as Pythium, so it's important to choose the hydroponic method best suited to spinach if this is something you want to grow. A vertical setup is a good choice for growing spinach if you want to avoid pathogens.

Kale: Kale is one of the most commonly used leafy greens in our diets, and Scotch kale is one of the most popular variations in the United States as it can be used in salads and smoothies or cooked as an added element to many recipes. Its high nutritional value makes it a popular ingredient for those who are health-conscious. It is known as one of the powerhouse vegetables and can be grown in warmer climates, which makes it a good option for hydroponic gardens. Although it can be sensitive to diseases and insects, there are ways to mitigate that.

Swiss chard: Swiss chard, or chard, is a leafy green high in vitamins and minerals. Sometimes also called spinach beet, it is a descendant of spinach. Swiss chard is a great choice for hydroponic gardeners as they are less susceptible to diseases and can be grown in warmer climates. With its long, leafy texture, it makes a delicious addition to many dishes.

Mustard greens: Mustard greens are a common delicacy in Africa and subtropical regions. They have a hot, spicy flavor and can be grown in cool temperatures, although they are able to withstand subtropical climates too. Mustard greens are good salad ingredients and can be used for braising as well. You can grow them in any hydroponic system.

Collard greens: Collard greens are related to kale and can withstand low temperatures. The best-tasting collard greens are grown in cooler regions, and gardeners love growing them. Collard greens grown hydroponically do best outdoors, but if you can provide enough space and maintain them properly, they will flourish indoors too.

Asian greens: These are considered the second-best powerhouse vegetable and belong to three different groups: turnips, Chinese mustard, and cabbage. This leafy green being a member of all three groups makes it the most compatible with hydroponic gardens. It is suited to different temperatures, making it easier for gardeners to plant them in their own setup.

EASIEST VEGETABLES FOR HYDROPONICS

Growing vegetables provides us with many options and opportunities in our gardens as well as in our everyday meals. Almost every kind of vegetable can be grown in a hydroponic system, and you can grow most of your leafy greens, salad veggies, and other vegetables in your own hydroponic garden if you understand their basic requirements. In order to harvest delicious fresh vegetables, you'll need to take steps to create the ideal atmosphere and environmental conditions for your plants. Here we'll look at some of the most common vegetables you can grow in your hydroponic garden and what each one needs to grow healthily and thrive:

Tomatoes: Tomatoes are ideal vegetables to grow in your hydroponic garden. You can grow both big and cherry tomatoes, and vertical setups are excellent for tomatoes as they are vine crops, making them space-saving as well as delicious! The ebb and flow method works very well for growing tomatoes, which grow best with a nutrient solution pH of around 5.5–6.5. Tomatoes also require plenty of sunlight and heat for optimal growth. Not only will you enjoy eating the tomatoes from your garden, but you'll enjoy the process of growing them as well.

Hot peppers: Hot peppers can be grown hydroponically with the deep water culture, ebb and flow, or drip systems. They require ample sunlight or equivalent light from other sources and their nutrient solution should maintain a pH of 6–6.8. Sometimes issues such as flower drops can happen, but overall, you'll get good, healthy produce in a shorter time period than soil-grown peppers.

Cucumbers: There are a variety of types of cucumbers you can choose to grow—you could even try growing them all at once! Whatever kind you want to grow for your salads, pickles, or other dishes, you can grow them in your own hydroponic garden. Make sure the pH ranges from 5.5–6 and the appropriate levels of temperature and heat are available. Cucumbers are high-yielding, and they grow faster in hydroponic gardens, so you can just sit back and let them do their thing. The ebb and flow method is a good option for cucumbers.

Beans: Beans have a range of options to choose from for growing in your hydroponic garden. You can grow lima, pole, string, or pinto beans. Try the drip system or ebb and flow method with a loose medium such as perlite or clay pebbles to grow your beans. You can use trellises for your string and pole beans to provide them with the maximum amount of sunlight. Keep the pH level around 6–6.3 for the best results, and give your beans some time to grow for a good harvest.

Sprouts and microgreens: Sprouts and microgreens are both good choices for hydroponic gardens as they need less space to grow and minimal heat and sunlight compared to other greens, and they grow faster than in soil-based gardening systems. Sprouts and microgreens are very nutritious and can be easily grown indoors. You do not have to worry about space, and like any other herb, they are cost-effective. Sprouts are produced from the germination of beans or seeds and have many uses in your daily meals. Some common varieties of sprouts are alfalfa sprouts, mung beans, fenugreek, chia, and sunflower sprouts. Microgreens are small plants that can be herbs or vegetables that are harvested at an earlier stage after the seedlings sprout but before the leaves start growing further. Microgreens can be kale, beets, broccoli, parsley, radishes, and similar vegetables or herbs.

Celery: Celery is considered a healthy vegetable and is often featured in salads and as an appetizer or snack because of its flavor and texture. Celery can be grown in your hydroponic garden with the ebb and flow system. Make sure the pH is between 5.7–6.

Green onions: Green onions, also known as scallions, are a good source of vitamins A, B, C, and K and protect us from viral infections and damage to our DNA. To grow green onions in your hydroponic garden, you'll first need to plant the seeds in a soil-filled pot and then transfer them to the hydroponic pots after they have sprouted.

Vegetables are vital sources of the vitamins and minerals we need to consume on a daily basis for a healthy diet. There is an old saying: "If you want to live long, eat vegetables!" With your hydroponic garden, you can grow these diet staples and incorporate them into all of your recipes, ensuring your family gets fresh, delicious food every day.

COMMON CHALLENGES

Earlier I mentioned that growing hydroponic herbs and vegetables can present some challenges when it comes to preventing diseases and pests that may attack your plants. Many herbs and vegetables are susceptible to these threats, but luckily there are strategies for dealing with them. In this section, we'll discuss common diseases as well as measures to prevent them from cropping up in your garden and how you can manage them if they do.

Downy Mildew

This disease is often found on arugula and basil. Black spots and yellow discoloration will appear on the top surface of the leaf.

Prevention

Keep the plant leaves dry and exposed to UV light. Make some space for the leaves and ensure good air circulation to avoid moisture residue. Remove any affected plants.

Treatment

Apply fungicides such as neem oil, hydrogen dioxide, potassium bicarbonate, or streptomyces.

Powdery Mildew

Powdery mildew is a fungal disease that can affect lettuce, rosemary, sage, and mint. Gray-white powder deposits will appear on the top surface of the leaf as well as the stem or flower of the plant.

Prevention

Allow adequate air circulation and control heat to avoid dry nights or humid days. Use horizontal air-flowing fans to allow proper air movement. Use varieties of the plant that are resistant to the disease.

Treatment

Apply *Bacillus amyloliquefaciens* like Triathlon BA, *Bacillus subtilis* like Companion, potassium bicarbonate, or streptomyces.

Gray Mold

Found on lettuce, rosemary, and other herbs, gray mold is another fungal disease. Brown or gray growth can be seen, and the stem becomes rotted and leaves dry out and become shriveled.

Prevention

Allow for proper ventilation and heat to avoid a humid atmosphere, especially at night. Remove any damaged or infected plants from the garden. Install fans that provide vertical air circulation.

Treatment

Fungicides such as *Bacillus subtilis* (Companion), *Bacillus amyloliquefaciens* (Triathlon BA), potassium bicarbonate, streptomyces, or hydrogen dioxide.

Pythium Root Rot

This is a fungus that mostly affects arugula, spinach, lettuce, or basil. Roots will look discolored. They tend to lose their outer layer and weak roots will appear. Yellow or brown coloring appears on roots and they fail to take in nutrients.

Prevention

Sanitize your tools and any floor mats at the entry to your garden. Test the water for any presence of Pythium species and treat the water. *Pythium aphanidermatum* and *Pythium myriotylum* grow faster in warm temperatures, so keep the water cool at 72 °F (22 °C).

Treatment

Apply biofungicides to prevent the growth of Pythium. You can find Pythium root rot fungicides available anywhere that provides greenhouse products.

White Mold

Also a fungus, white mold affects lettuce and sometimes cilantro. White-brown lesions will appear on many parts of the plant, and the roots will begin to rot. Cotton-like deposits called mycelium also appear.

Prevention

Plant lettuce in dry conditions and avoid damp surfaces. Maintain good airflow and spacing between plants. Avoid bringing damaged or infected plants inside if they were previously outside.

Treatment

Apply fungicides such as *Bacillus amyloliquefaciens* (e.g., Triathlon BA, Double Nickel), *Bacillus subtilis* (e.g., Cease, Companion), or streptomyces.

In this chapter, we've talked all about vegetables and leafy greens you can grow in your hydroponic garden, including some of the best vegetables to grow and how to manage challenges that may arise. In the next chapter, we'll discuss herbs and how to best grow fresh, aromatic, and flavorful herbs in your hydroponic garden.

7

HERBAL HYDROS

> *All those spices and herbs in your spice rack can do more than provide calorie-free, natural flavorings to enhance and make food delicious. They're also an incredible source of antioxidants and help rev up your metabolism and improve your health at the same time.*

— SUZANNE SOMERS

Herbs are essential to our diet and health, and hydroponically grown herbs will give you an additional quality of freshness and taste. An herb is a "plant or plant part valued for its medicinal, savory, or aromatic qualities" (Merriam-Webster, n.d.-b). There is a huge variety of herbs, including basil, parsley, alfalfa, and many more.

Herbal hydros, or herbs grown in hydroponic gardens, will provide you with faster-growing and more aromatic herbs. No matter what kind of herbs you want, it is possible to grow them in the right environment and conditions. You have to take into account factors like pH, total dissolved solids, and electrical conductivity of your hydroponic solution for the best outcomes. Herbs are great ingredients for medicines, cooking, and oils. Before you go forward with your herb garden, take note of the following important conditions:

Nutrients and water: Herbs require both water and nutrient solutions that are of good quality to ensure the best growth. The solution must have a good ratio of phosphorus and nitrogen content. Electrical conductivity should be between 1–1.16 Siemens per meter and have a concentration of 800–1,200 ppm (parts per million) of total dissolved solids. The best pH for herbs is 5.5–6.4. With all these parameters at their optimum levels, you will have a good hydroponic herb garden in no time.

Type of hydroponic system: There are many options for hydroponic systems you can use for your herb garden, including an 8-column or 12-column hydroponic system. You can find these and more at any gardening store specifically for hydroponics. The 8-column tower contains clay pellets as a medium and allows good air circulation for the herbs. This system can be used indoors or outdoors. The 12-column tower is used mainly indoors and contains a siphon that helps the water flow downward to allow oxygen to reach the roots, helping your herbs grow better and healthier. Using hydroponics to grow herbs makes them tastier and more aromatic, and they grow faster than those grown in soil.

Lighting: The best option for lighting in your herb garden is a T5 fluorescent tube light that gives off a temperature of 6,500 Kelvin. These are high-output lights and can be placed up to 12 inches above the garden. Another great lighting option is T12 fluorescent lights which can be used at different growth stages, such as when you're planting seeds and during the seedling stage. On the other hand, HID and LED are lighting systems that are used in larger operations.

Besides these conditions, there are many tips you can follow to get even better results with your hydroponic herbs. Here are some points to keep in mind:

- Ensure you have a good drainage system in place for your herbs as a wet surface will not allow oxygen to reach the roots.
- Ensure that the atmosphere is not hot and dry, which may cause the plants to become weak, making them more susceptible to pests such as mites, aphids, or whiteflies.
- Keep the daytime temperature between 65–70 °F (18–21 °C), and night temperatures can be around 55–60 °F (13–16 °C).

BEST HERBS FOR HYDROPONICS

There are many flavorful and multiuse herbs, and most of them can be easily grown in your hydroponic garden. Some of the best of these are cilantro, lemon balm, oregano, mint, basil, thyme, watercress, chamomile, lavender, and alfalfa. Mint, lemon balm, lavender, and chamomile all have various health and medical uses, and watercress, oregano, and basil make good garnishes and greatly improve the flavors of your dishes. Alfalfa can be used for both purposes.

In addition to their uses in cooking and medicines, herbs also have many other purposes in both their raw and processed forms. Herbs are a source of vitamins, fiber, calcium, magnesium, and potassium, but the levels and combinations of these things may vary among different types of herbs. Some herbs have even proven helpful in curbing cognitive decline associated with dementia and Alzheimer's disease (Deering, 2019). Be cautious, however, as there are some herbs that should not be used with infants or children as they may not have been tested for safety issues.

TOP HERBS FOR COOKING

Using herbs in your cooking adds flavor and provides a source of vitamins and minerals. There are several herbs that can improve your culinary creations and help keep you and your family healthy.

Cilantro: Cilantro is very common and can be used in all kinds of cuisines, but it was first used for cooking in the Mediterranean. Cilantro and coriander come from different parts of the same plant. Cilantro not only gives a tangy taste and smell to your food but has the added quality of cleansing your bloodstream of toxic metals.

Lemon balm: Lemon balm is a great flavor contributor to many dishes, and you can also use it to make a delicious and refreshing herbal tea. It is a popular essential oil, so it can be diffused to add a clean, crisp aroma to your home. Lemon balm plants grow up to 2 feet tall—sometimes taller! It is grown almost everywhere around the world but is originally from Europe.

Oregano: Oregano originated in Greece and is one of the most flavorful and common ingredients used by chefs today. This herb, or microgreen, is not a fast-growing plant, so you'll have to be patient before harvesting. It has an earthy smell and taste that complements the flavors of foods such as pizza, salads, soups, steaks, and marinara sauce. When growing oregano in a hydro-ponic system, use high-output fluorescent tube lights and plant them with tomatoes, peppers, or basil as companion plants. A major benefit of growing oregano in your hydroponic garden is that it repels aphids!

Mint: Mint adds a cool, refreshing flavor to any dish and is often used in Middle Eastern cooking, including lamb chops, vegetable dishes, and soups. Mint was one of the first plants to be grown hydroponically, and in fact, it's relatively easy to grow and maintain and tends to do better when it's grown hydroponically. It can even be transferred and planted in other parts of your garden. By cutting smaller stems right where they shoot off from the main stem, you can harvest a large amount of this herb. In order to plant mint, you'll want to use a medium such as coco coir and give it up to 16 days to germinate. You can even transfer the germinated seedlings to your hydroponic garden later.

Basil: Basil can be easily grown hydroponically and is used in many dishes, especially in the Mediterranean. It gives your food a beautiful aroma and contains vitamins and calcium. Basil enhances the flavor of salads, pizza, pasta, and many of your favorite comfort foods. Many Vietnamese, Indonesian, and Thai cuisines include this flavorful herb because of its great aromatic qualities. There are multiple kinds of basil, including sweet basil, cinnamon basil, and lemon basil. You can create many basil plants from a single basil plant by using cutting and grafting techniques. Grafting is a type of plant propagation where you snip off a part of one plant and attach it to your hydroponic plant stem. This is done by slicing a small diagonal cut into the stem of the plant you are grafting onto, or the "rootstock," then you make another cut going straight down the stem. You then cut the end of the snipped stem diagonally to match the cut you made on the rootstock stem. You'll then insert the snipped stem into the rootstock stem, matching up the cuts, and secure the stems with twine or grafting wax (Neveln,

2015). It takes up to 7 days for a basil seed to germinate, and it does best at temperatures between 70–73 °F (21–23 °C). Basil grows well in mediums such as perlite, vermiculite, foam substrates, peat moss, or coconut fiber.

Thyme: Thyme is part of the mint family and originally came from Europe and the Mediterranean. It has an earthy taste and is aromatic, which makes it an ideal addition to many dishes. Both garden thyme and lemon thyme are commonly used in cooking, adding wonderful flavors to foods such as vegetables, lamb, pork, and fish. Thyme can also be grown through propagation, and when it's grown in your hydroponic system, you do not need to worry about fertilizing. It's important to note, though, that thyme may be susceptible to pests such as mites or whiteflies.

Watercress: Watercress is often used in salad dressings, soups, or as a garnish to put the finishing touch on delicious dishes. You can eat the leaves by snipping them off the stem. This herb can be grown to harvest, and it can be easily transferred to other locations through propagation. As the name suggests, watercress grows best in water, and you can use a good medium or root plug to plant these herbs.

Marjoram: Marjoram is often compared to oregano due to its quality of adding flavor and aroma to your food, but many professional chefs who use all kinds of herbs in their cooking note that they do have some differences. Marjoram originated from Egypt and was even used in some of their religious ceremonies. Marjoram is a fragrant spice that complements meat dishes very well and is sometimes referred to as the "meat herb." Marjoram can be grown in warm temperatures and grows up to 10 inches tall. Marjoram is ideal for hydroponic gardens because it's easy to snip off a stem and plant the cutting.

TOP HERBS FOR MEDICINES

Herbs can effortlessly elevate any dish, but there are also herbs that are equally useful when it comes to making medicines and ointments. They are great for everyday use and can make life a little easier. Instead of running to the pharmacy, you can turn to your hydroponic garden for many home remedies. Here are some common medicinal herbs that you may want to grow in your hydroponic garden:

Mint: Like many herbs, mint can be used to help relieve a number of ailments such as irritable bowel syndrome (IBS), gastrointestinal problems, allergies, and more. There are several species of mint, and the most common are spearmint and peppermint. This herb has numerous uses commercially and at home as a remedy or incorporated into an ointment.

Lemon balm: Lemon balm can help in calming stress, anxiety, or indigestion. As a medicine, it can also be used to manage insomnia, anxiety, and even herpes. As the name "balm" implies, it was once used as a healing herb to treat wounds and even bites from venomous insects. If you want to use lemon balm for medicinal purposes, look into any possible side effects that could result from interactions with other medicines you may be taking.

Cilantro: Cilantro has several vitamins and minerals that enhance your nutritional intake. It also contains antioxidants, which play an important role in fighting many illnesses. It is best to grow your cilantro from its seed rather than transferring it from another pot. Pick the cilantro from the plant before the flowers begin to grow or it will become bitter in taste. Cilantro has been known to help with

- improving heart health.
- supplying antioxidants.
- controlling blood sugar levels.
- maintaining fungal balance.
- reducing harmful organisms.
- improving brain health.
- improving bone health.
- aiding the digestive system (Dr. Group, DC, 2017).

Basil: Basil has many medicinal uses, such as treating inflammation, and it also contains antioxidants. Antioxidants help to remove oxidative stress in your body, which can cause many illnesses such as cancer, heart disease, and diabetes. This herb is used in ointments for snake bites and can help reduce cold symptoms and nasal passage inflammation. Basil can also be useful in

- reducing blood sugar.
- supporting cardiovascular health.
- supporting mental health.
- fighting infections.
- slowing down the aging process.
- supporting liver health (WebMD Editorial Contributors, 2020).

Chamomile: There are two types of chamomile: Roman and German. The flowers from this plant can be dried and made into herbal medicines to use for many ailments, and it makes a good herbal tea. Chamomile can also help to relieve stress, reduce indigestion, and relieve skin inflammation and irritation.

Lavender: Lavender has a soothing scent and is often used to help promote relaxation. It is not just beautifully aromatic but has also been known to relieve anxiety, reduce stress, and help with insomnia. It can also be used as an antiseptic.

Alfalfa: Alfalfa is a sprout that is used as animal feed and supplement for your food. It is actually a legume but is often used as an herb. It contains many minerals and vitamins and is an excellent addition to salads. As a medicine, alfalfa can treat nausea, morning sickness, kidney issues, and urinary problems.

COMMON CHALLENGES

Hydroponic herbs have amazing qualities for cooking, medicines, and home sanitization. Among their many uses, herbs can provide an earthy, sweet, and relaxing aroma and atmosphere to your home. In order to grow a healthy and bountiful hydroponic herb garden, there are a few things you'll want to keep in mind.

Know your herbs: It's important to be knowledgeable about any herb species you choose to plant. If you can't provide the ideal environment and growing conditions for a given plant, you likely won't get the results you're hoping for, so take some time to research and learn about any herbs you think you might want to grow in your hydroponic garden. Look for guidance on mediums, growing instruments, lighting, and any other requirements for each kind of herb you want to grow in order to achieve the best results possible.

Maintain proper pH: The pH of your hydroponic solution is incredibly important when growing herbs. If the pH is too low or too high, not only will the growth of the herbs be affected, but so will some of their natural qualities. Some herbs are more sensitive to changes in pH than others and may not grow properly if the pH isn't just right. You can ensure your nutrient solutions are at the right pH by using a good-quality, reliable pH meter—either digital or liquid testing kits—and checking on your plants regularly. You can find pH meters and testing kits online or in any gardening store. You may need to use supplements to lower or increase the pH, and these can be found from the same retailers.

Check the system: Check your hydroponic system for leaks or other malfunctions as well as whether any adjustments or repairs are needed. If any valves or pipelines aren't working properly, your garden won't be able to function optimally, and you'll be less likely to achieve the outcomes you're working so hard for. If there's not a lot of room in the reservoir, consider keeping the used nutrient solution stored somewhere else so that you can use it again and create a little more space in the reservoir. Another problem you may encounter is overgrown roots blocking the holes and passages within the system, so try to keep them clean and clear of debris.

Use the right solution: Nutrient solutions are very important for your hydroponic herbs. It's helpful to keep a record of the pH, electrical conductivity, and concentrations of various nutrients to avoid any problems during the growing period. Every herb requires a particular amount of these parameters to grow healthily. For example, basil needs a pH of 5.5—6.5, a conductivity of 10–16 cF, and a concentration of dissolved solids of 700–1,120 ppm (Jagdish, 2021a).

Maintain temperature: The temperature is another critical factor to watch out for when growing herbs hydroponically, especially indoors. You have to maintain a temperature that allows for good oxygen levels and air circulation in and around your hydroponic garden. You'll have to do some research to know what temperatures are optimal for every kind of herb you want in your garden so they get the right amount of oxygen. High temperatures and low oxygen levels are the worst combination as this initiates the right conditions for root rot and other diseases.

Provide adequate oxygen: It is vital for enough oxygen to reach the roots of herb plants to create conditions that allow for the best growth possible. If roots do not get enough oxygen, diseases such as root rot may appear. The ebb and flow method facilitates sufficient oxygen flow to the roots when the water flows out. This gives the roots a chance to breathe between cycles, which supports healthy growth as well.

Focus on sanitization: Sanitization has been a priority for everyone ever since the COVID-19 pandemic started. We have learned how to incorporate sanitizing our hands and the items we handle often into our daily routines. Plants are like humans, meaning they are more likely to be healthy and thrive if they are clean, so keeping your hydroponic garden as clean as possible to avoid germs, pests, and diseases that can inhibit plant growth is essential. You can try some of the following techniques:

- Sanitize the reservoir and net pots.
- Keep the floor or ground surrounding your hydroponic garden clean and dry.
- Sanitize your garden tools.
- Sanitize and clean the equipment in the hydroponic system.
- Dispose of any plant waste or debris from your garden.

You may not encounter problems growing herbs in your hydroponic garden often, but it is best to be prepared as issues can arise suddenly and should be addressed promptly. Help prepare yourself by doing research to understand more about growing herbs in hydroponic systems and take note of the pros and cons for the best results for your time and effort.

It can be helpful to record the parameters you use for growing your herbs—or any plant—so you can see what works and what doesn't. Below is an example of a log book you can maintain throughout your gardening process:

Date	pH	Temperature	Nutrient solution	EC	TDS	DO	Sanitation date	Nutrient change date

All of these parameters should be recorded with the appropriate meters or equipment, all of which are available online or in any gardening or aquaculture store. When you search online, be strategic about your search phrases; for example, if you want to search for a TDS meter, you'll get the best results for your purposes if you search something like "TDS meter for hydroponics."

We have seen how useful herbs are for us in our cooking and medicinally, and we've discussed how you can grow the best possible herbs in your hydroponic garden. Next, we'll talk about even more plants that have hidden qualities and uses.

8

PRETTY LOVELY

“ *If you look the right way, you can see that the whole world is a garden.*

— FRANCES HODGSON BURNETT

F lowers are not only for decorating and planting in your garden to look beautiful, but they are symbols of peace and happiness. Flowers give our homes a tranquil feeling and add a pop of life and color to any room. In this chapter, we're going to explore the best flowers to grow in your hydroponic garden.

BEST FLOWERS FOR HYDROPONICS

A number of the best flowers you can find at the store are grown hydroponically. Growing flowers hydroponically can give you faster yields—up to 2–5 times higher than soil-grown flowers (Bulla, 2022). Hydroponics also allows you to grow flowers even if you have limited space. Let's take a closer look at some of the best flowers you can grow in your hydroponic garden.

Daffodils: Daffodils are beautiful, so much so that the famous poet, William Wordsworth, wrote a poem about them. This flower can be grown in your hydroponic garden as long as the environment is cool and dry. If the flowers become wilted, you do not have to do anything but let them recover with some care and appropriate nutrition. These beautiful flowers originated in the Mediterranean and are now grown all over the world.

Amaryllis: Amaryllises are big beautiful flowers that can brighten any room with their decorative petals. Their flowers bloom from large bulbs, and they are ideal for hydroponic gardens. You can use the Kratky and deep water culture methods for this plant to allow the roots to soak in the water. Amaryllises have a variety of cultivars you can choose for your hydroponic garden. A cultivar is a kind of plant that is purposefully grown for its desirable traits and reproduced to preserve and replicate those traits. Make sure the amaryllis bulb is kept dry while the roots are in the nutrient solution. This flower blossoms at temperatures 70–75 °F (21–24 °C). Note that your nutrient solution must have a low nitrogen content.

Hydroponic orchid grown in partial water and air

Orchids: Orchids are an especially elegant flower with thousands of species, and their beauty is very special to many gardeners and flower lovers (Bulla, 2022). Orchids are called "epiphytes," which means their roots grow upward instead of down and their roots need to be partially exposed to air and not constantly dipped in stagnant water. Many gardeners are changing their orchid gardens over to hydroponic systems as they have proven to be more efficient and manageable. Orchids need a humid atmosphere to grow, and their roots will absorb nutrients mostly from the atmosphere. This process is somewhat distinct from many flowering plants. Make sure the tips of the roots are exposed to air and light.

Peace lily: Peace lilies are flowers that stand out with their bold white-and-green appearance. They're some of the best flowers to grow in your hydroponic garden, but be sure to avoid adding chlorine to the water as it might hinder their growth. The Kratky method is a great option for this flower, and it will not take up much space; however, you want to make sure only the roots are dipped in the nutrient solution. The best part of growing a peace lily is that it makes a beautiful addition to any room in your home when kept in a crystal jar or vase.

Iris: Irises are a bold and beautiful flower to brighten your garden and home, and Egyptians and Indians have been planting this flower since ancient times. The inflorescence—the part that blooms—grows with three sepals, three petals, and three stigmas that produce pollen. They can easily grow in water ponds, making them another great flower to grow in a hydroponic garden. Some species of iris grow best in hydroponics by directly adding seeds. Species such as *Iris variegata*, *Iris versicolor*, or *Iris tectorum* are good options. The two most common types of iris are bulbous and rhizomatous. Make sure only the roots dip in the water and not the bulb.

Carnations: Carnations are another flower that does well in hydroponic systems, and there are a variety of carnation species available. These strong and sweet-smelling flowers were once known as "divine flowers" by the ancient Greeks. Carnations have a long blooming time, and you can use the ebb and flow method, deep water culture, or drip system for this plant. These flowers grow well indoors, and around 5–10 hours of light is enough for them to grow properly. The temperature should range from 55–64 °F (13–18 °C) during the day, and at night, you can keep the temperature around 41–44 °F (5–7 °C).

Freesia: Freesia is a sweet-smelling flower to grow in your hydroponic garden. It blooms in several colors, including purple, yellow, white, orange, and red. It has long-lined leaves and the plant is inflorescent, meaning that it will blossom. Keep the bulbs of this flower out of the nutrient solution, allowing only the roots to touch it, and keep them at a steady 86 °F (30 °C) if you want them to bloom. Because Freesia originates from South Africa, it is accustomed to a warmer climate.

Hydroponic chrysanthemums

Chrysanthemums: Chrysanthemums are another gorgeous flower that will adorn your hydroponic garden with its blaze of bright yellow. As the official flower of Japan and a religious symbol in the United States, the chrysanthemum is not only lovely but also significant in many ways. Chrysanthemums, sometimes referred to as mums, are "photoperiodic," which means they grow based on the amount of light they receive in a day. In order to blossom to their fullest potential, mums need around 7–12 hours of direct daylight, so set your hydroponic system's grow lights to around 9 hours each day. It's important to note that chrysanthemums tend to be vulnerable to Pythium, which we discussed in Chapter 6, so you want to make sure to cut them at least every 2 years in case the disease has invaded to keep it from causing irreversible damage to the plant.

Hyacinth: Hyacinths are another sweet-smelling flower that can be grown hydroponically, and they do particularly well when grown using the Kratky method. Hyacinths are easy to care for as you can keep one in a container with the right nutrient solution and let it do its thing—but make sure there is enough nutrient solution for the plant to survive. You need to take care of the hyacinth bulbs as they can become weak, and it is best to cut off the flowering part, or inflorescence, so the bulb gets enough nutrients from the solution. Hyacinths have a short blooming time and cannot withstand cold temperatures.

Gerbera daisies: Gerbera daisies are tropical in origin and grow in a wide variety of vibrant colors, including pink, red, yellow, and white, so even just a few will add an eye-catching element to your garden. Gerbera daisies prefer indirect sunlight and cooler temperatures—around 40–70 °F (4–21 °C)—so using diffused light to grow them in your hydroponic garden will help avoid burning their leaves.

OTHER PLANTS FOR YOUR HYDROPONIC GARDEN

There are many options for plants you can grow in your hydroponic garden—herbs, fruits, vegetables, and flowers. Houseplants are another type of plant that can be grown hydroponically, and they serve the dual purpose of adding a pop of natural decor as well as purifying the air inside your home.

In order to grow a healthy, flourishing hydroponic garden, it's essential to know the needs, benefits, and challenges of each plant you are growing. Each plant will differ when it comes to the optimal time to plant, when to cut the flower, what nutrient solution is best, and what kind of medium you should use to get the best results. No matter which houseplant you choose for your hydroponic garden, you must be able to cultivate them by simply cutting and transferring them to your hydroponic system, although some plants may require a little more work than others. Let's look at some of the different kinds of houseplants you can grow hydroponically.

Dragon tree: With its pointy leaves, this plant adds a dramatic look to any room. It's easy to take care of and can be propagated and planted in your hydroponic garden. Originating in Madagascar, they do best in warmer temperatures between 70–80 °F (21–27 °C). If you're an animal lover as well as a plant lover, be mindful of where you place this plant because the dragon tree can be harmful if eaten by your pets.

Chinese money plant: The Chinese money plant is another kind of plant you can grow hydroponically. It originated from Australia, Costa Rica, and small islands in the Pacific Ocean and prefers to grow in humid tropical climates. They can produce seeds and be planted as cuttings in your hydroponic garden.

Philodendron: Philodendron can be grown by transferring cuttings as well as using seeds. This is a climbing plant and often has aerial roots that point upward. These plants are native to Central and South American tropical forests and can withstand humidity and warm temperatures, around 68–82 °F (20–28 °C).

Chinese evergreen: Chinese evergreen can be grown naturally from seed, or there are multiple methods of propagation that will work, such as propagation by division or by sowing and tissue culture. The roots grow faster when grown hydroponically, and the plant looks much more ornamental. Ensure healthy growth by changing this plant's water frequently. Chinese evergreen plants originated from tropical Africa, Malaysia, and the Philippines, so it grows best in a warm, humid climate.

Devil's ivy: Devil's ivy is a perennial climbing or trailing plant that has beautiful leaves. This plant grows in warm, humid climates and prefers full light, though it can tolerate cooler temperatures and lower lighting levels. Devil's ivy has the handy quality of removing dampness from the environment.

Spider plant: A spider plant is one of the easiest plants to grow and is an excellent choice for hydroponic beginners. This plant can be grown by cutting or from seed. This plant is easy to maintain as it only needs water and medium light to grow. Though spider plants are commonly grown in soil, it's actually quite easy to transfer them to a water medium; the biggest difference is that you have to add nutrients to the water. Be sure to change the water regularly as you do not want any buildup of minerals or salts.

Arrowhead vine: Arrowhead vines can be grown by transferring cuttings to your hydroponic system. This plant is another popular houseplant that originated from tropical regions and does not need direct sunlight to thrive. This plant can grow very well indoors or outdoors and does best in spring, summer, and fall.

LIMITATIONS IN TYPES OF PLANTS GROWN HYDROPONICALLY

We have covered the many options hydroponic gardening offers as far as what kinds of herbs, vegetables, fruits, flowers, and house-plants you can grow in your garden. Unfortunately, there are some plants that do not do as well in hydroponic systems. The characteristics and environmental requirements of these plants make them different from plants that can be easily grown hydroponically. In this section, we'll talk a little bit about these types of plants and what makes them less-than-ideal for your hydroponic garden.

Hydroponically grown plants have to be suited to a water-based environment that depends solely on the nutrients and minerals provided in the hydroponic system. In addition to this, there are other factors that can preclude a plant from thriving in a hydroponic system, such as space, root structure, demand for resources, and maintenance. Let's look at some of these plants and the reasons they are not as well-suited for hydroponic setups.

- **Root crops:** Root crops such as carrots, radishes, turnips, and potatoes cannot be easily grown hydroponically because the root is the edible part of the vegetable. Some can be grown with adaptations made for temperature, pH, or nutrients. If you do want to try growing root crops hydroponically, the ebb and flow system is your best bet.
- **Plants that produce large fruit:** Large fruits such as cantaloupe, watermelon, and squash are difficult to grow hydroponically because they need extra support to keep them upright and strong. If you still want to take the chance, then you may have to use something such as

cardboard or a raft—a wooden structure that floats—to hold them up.

- **Trees:** Trees need a huge space, especially once they have grown to their full size. They need adequate air, CO_2, and light to survive compared to plants grown hydroponically. You can grow fruit trees in your hydroponic garden, but only if they are dwarf species that have been grafted and can grow in smaller spaces. If you do plant a tree in your hydroponic garden you will eventually have to transfer it outdoors to allow for optimal growth.
- **Vining and bush plants:** Plants such as zucchini, corn, climbers, and others are not suitable to grow in hydroponic setups due to the large root systems they have that allow them to take in sufficient nutrients and minerals. Also, these plants tend to spread out horizontally as they grow, which can create space issues.

All of the flowers and plants discussed in this chapter have their own requirements for nutrition and healthy growth as well as unique challenges. In the next chapter, we'll take a look at some of the challenges you might face on your hydroponic gardening journey and how you can deal with them to keep your garden growing.

9

CHALLENGES

> *If you have a positive attitude and constantly strive to give your best effort, eventually you will overcome your immediate problems and find you are ready for greater challenges.*

— PAT RILEY

When you're pursuing a goal, many challenges can present themselves along the way, and all types of gardening—agricultural, organic, aquaponics, and hydroponics—come with their own sets of unique challenges. Hydroponics is considered the cleanest and most environmentally friendly way to grow crops, so if you want a sustainable way to grow your garden that reduces pollution and the misuse of resources, then hydroponics is the right choice, but there are still challenges that may arise with this method. Let's talk about some of the potential obstacles you may encounter when working with your hydroponic garden.

THINGS TO WATCH OUT FOR

We talked earlier about the many aspects you'll want to consider before beginning your hydroponic garden, but let's briefly recap here.

- **Cost of the system:** Depending on the kinds of plants you want to grow and the equipment you need for the type of system you choose to use for your hydroponic garden, the costs can vary greatly. It's important to set a budget for yourself before making any big plans so you know what you're working with before you even get started. You may have to compromise and only choose one or two kinds of plants to start with and add on as you go.
- **Power connection:** A fully equipped hydroponic system requires a constant source of electricity. Power is needed for pumps, grow lights, and fans or air conditioning, especially in indoor gardens. Therefore, if you cannot provide this constant supply of electricity, it may be difficult to grow your plants effectively, especially if you have an active hydroponic system that needs support from air pumps and air conditioning to keep your plants growing, which requires a continuous power supply to keep working.
- **Maintenance:** As we have discussed in great detail, there are certain parameters that should be monitored in your hydroponic nutrient solution such as pH, electrical conductivity, total dissolved solids, and temperature. In order to keep a controlled environment, these parameters have to be steadily maintained. It's also important to keep your setup clean and be on the lookout for clogs, leaks, or

blockages in the system. Lastly, you'll need to flush out the nutrient solution and refill it periodically.

- **Managing waterborne diseases:** Waterborne diseases are common, so it's critical to take some precautions to avoid them, such as using filtered water and regularly flushing used nutrient solution to add fresh solution. Once you notice a waterborne disease in your system, you'll want to take immediate action to remedy it or risk losing your plants.

These problems may sound difficult to deal with at first, but once you begin your own hydroponic garden, everything will fall into place and seem more manageable. The best way to mitigate problems in your hydroponic garden is to follow requirements and recommendations for your particular plants and system and to make sure the entire system is set up properly.

TOP 15 PROBLEMS AND THEIR SOLUTIONS

There is no learning without making mistakes in life. Similarly, when you want to start a new project such as hydroponic gardening, you will have to go through certain phases of trial and error in order to establish a great hydroponic system. Every misstep and miscalculation is an opportunity to learn and develop your skills as a hydroponic gardener. Though they can be frustrating, there are solutions to every problem that may arise in your garden. Now we'll talk about some of the most common problems and how to resolve them so you can successfully grow your hydroponic garden.

1. Inadequate lighting:

One of the most important aspects of setting up your hydroponic garden is selecting the right lighting that will support your plants at all stages of growth. If you choose a lighting system that does not provide the right intensity and temperature, you might end up growing fewer healthy plants, thus inadequate lighting systems may cause poor yield of vegetables and fruits.

Solution: The best way to avoid this problem is to choose the perfect lighting for your plants that will support their growth in the first place. For example, T5 fluorescent grow lights or LED lights will give you the best results overall. You'll need to do some research about which lights are best for your particular plants, and you want to avoid choosing an LED that will not emit the exact wavelength your plants need. Remember, poor quality means poor outcomes. You can also calculate the square footage of your hydroponic garden canopy, or the upper layer of the hydroponic plants. This can be done by measuring the length (L) and width (W) of the room or space of your hydroponic garden in feet. Multiply the length by the width to find the area of the space and then multiply the value by 50 watts, which will give you the watt coverage for your hydroponic garden area. This value will give you an idea of the amount of power, or wattage, the lighting you choose should have in order to best support your plants' growth. This can vary among different lights too; for example, fluorescent lights may need 5 times more wattage than high-intensity discharge (HID) lights (*Wattage Calculator*, n.d.).

2. Choosing the wrong medium:

As we discussed in Chapter 3, there is a wide variety of growing mediums to choose from, both organic and inorganic. There are mediums that help plants grow in a dry atmosphere, while others leave water pools at the bottom. Some mediums are highly absorbent, and some are not. Thus, it's important to understand the needs of each of your plants and select the mediums that will best meet those needs.

Solution: Take some time to research different kinds of mediums and each of your plant types as certain mediums are recommended for specific plants. Knowing how each medium works can help you make your choice for your plants. If you're unsure, you can seek the advice of an experienced hydroponic gardener or that of a hydroponic supplier or greenhouse employee who will know which medium is best for your plants.

3. Not monitoring pH:

The pH level of your hydroponic solution can vary based on a number of factors, such as a change in temperature or absorption rates or too much evaporation occurring. It can be easy to miss these things if you don't closely monitor your nutrient solution.

Solution: In order to catch any changes in the pH of your plants' nutrient solutions, use an accurate pH meter to check and record their pH levels two to three times a week. With careful pH monitoring, you can ensure your plants' nutrient solutions have a pH balance that is just right for them and that the whole system is working smoothly.

4. Failing to monitor EC, TDS, or nutrient concentration:

It is essential to monitor the electrical conductivity, nutrient concentration (in ppm), and total dissolved solids in your nutrient solution every now and then. This will help you keep track of the amount of toxic substances or additional minerals present in the nutrient solution so you can make sure the concentration of minerals is just right for your plant's requirements.

Solution: Monitoring your nutrient solution's concentration in ppm, EC, and TDS is important at the beginning of growing your hydroponic plants and throughout all of their growth stages. Check and record these values every two weeks if possible. This will tell you a lot about the composition of the solution and its contents; however, it's important to note that this will not tell you which minerals or salts are present, so the best course of action is to replace the nutrient solution with a fresh mixture. This will ensure there are no unwanted substances or deficiencies in the nutrient solution.

5. Nonideal fertilizers:

One big difference between soil-grown plants and hydroponic plants is the nutrient source. Soil contains some trace nutrients, whereas, in hydroponics, you can add the nutrients separately and combine each solution to the needs of each specific plant. In order to select the right nutrients, you'll need to know the micro- and macronutrient requirements for all your plants.

Solution: It's helpful to keep a store of the nutrients your plants need on hand and ready to use. A good option is to buy packages that contain two- or three-part solutions. You can easily adjust the nutrient solution according to each plant's requirements.

6. Inconvenient hydroponic system:

Hydroponic systems are the most sustainable and environmentally friendly systems for gardening, but it does take a certain amount of time and effort on your part to grow a well-planned and productive garden. You'll want to plan your hydroponic system in such a way that it does not feel cumbersome or tiring at the end of the day. It is a simple technique of growing plants with only water and a nutrient solution, but in order for it to be as efficient as it can be, you'll want to find the right location for it. You'll also want to store your hydroponic equipment so that it is easily within reach when you need something.

Solution: To create the most convenient hydroponic system, you'll want to make a detailed plan for your setup in advance. Be sure to take things such as available space for the system itself, workspace surfaces, storage space for equipment and supplies, power and water sources, and natural lighting into account when planning your hydroponic garden. You'll want to keep things relatively close so that no matter what you need, it's within reach. Your equipment should be situated near the water source to help you clean and reassemble the system easily. If you build your own DIY system, keep in mind the utilities you will need when your hydroponic system is set up and fully working. We'll talk much more about DIY hydroponic systems in the next chapter.

7. Lack of cleanliness:

A dirty, cluttered hydroponic gardening area is more susceptible to developing diseases and attracting pests. Another common issue in messier hydroponic gardens is the growth of algae. All of this will negatively affect the growth and health of your plants and be detrimental to your garden's overall results. There may be good bacteria as well as bad bacteria present in your hydroponic system; your job is to stop the growth of pathogens, especially indoors as these are more harmful.

Solution: Make sure your hydroponic garden and its surroundings are clean and sanitized as much as possible. A clean environment will help you keep a clean system, which also helps prevent pests and diseases from invading your garden. You'll also want to perform regular cleaning and maintenance on your reservoir, pipes, and valves—every two weeks is a good rule of thumb.

8. System leaks:

System leaks can happen when the reservoir becomes too full and the nutrient solution leaks or overflows out the top. Sometimes a root mass can block the passage the nutrient solution needs to flow through and cause the water to overflow—this problem will occur in the nutrient film system if you don't regularly clear out debris left in the solution.

Solution: First, check the valves and the whole hydroponic system before starting the process of planting your crops. You'll also want to check if there are any clogs or plant debris that might cause a blockage in the nutrient solution. Make sure to use a good-sized reservoir that will be able to support the volume of water needed for your plants.

9. Broken pumps or pipes:

Apart from monitoring your plants and nutrient solution, you also want to regularly monitor your hydroponic equipment, including air pumps, pipes, and other small parts that could affect the whole system. A system that isn't fully and properly functioning could experience blockages or breaks in the flow of water or nutrients to the plants. For example, an aeroponic system could have problems with debris getting clogged in the nozzles of the connecting tubes or pipes. Another issue you might run into is an air pump that stops working correctly, making it difficult for oxygen to reach the plants, which can result in poor health of the roots.

Solution: Check the entire system periodically for any breaks or clogs in the pipes. You might even consider getting an air pump that will alert you when there is a blockage.

10. Forgetting to flush and refill the system:

Flushing and refilling the nutrient solution in your hydroponic garden is very important for keeping your plants growing healthily. When you notice the solution looking cloudy or dirty, you'll want to change it out for fresh, clean solution. If you go too long without changing the solution, you might create problems that will persist throughout the growing stage, so be sure to monitor and change your nutrient solutions regularly.

Solution: Make sure to regularly flush out the used nutrients and minerals to add a new batch of nutrient solution to your hydroponic system. Keep a record of how often you do this so that you don't unintentionally wait too long. A clean environment produces healthy plants and crops.

11. Not monitoring plant health:

You want to learn as much about your plants before planting them as possible, including what they should look like when they're healthy and what they'll look like if they become unhealthy. You'll also want to be aware of any health issues that certain plants are prone to so you can keep an eye out for them.

Solution: Monitor your plants' health from the beginning of their growth stages. If you detect any diseases or pests, take action to remedy the issue as soon as possible. Check for any changes in your plant's growth or signs of potential problems and provide any additional supplements or pesticides needed right away.

12. Not meeting your plants' needs:

As we know, every kind of plant has unique requirements for things like pH and nutrients, so it's inevitable that every new hydroponic gardener will make a mistake or miscalculation that affects a plant's growth. If this happens to you, don't be too hard on yourself! Mistakes are opportunities to learn and do better the next time. If, for example, you used the wrong type of nutrient at the wrong time, you'll know what you need to do differently next time.

Solution: The best way to keep track of what worked and what didn't is to keep a log of all your plants and note down their requirements at each stage of growth. One great way to give your-self a full overview of your plants' growth cycles is to take pictures and videos of their progress. This can help you avoid future mistakes with your hydroponic plants and crops.

13. Nutrient deficiencies:

Issues relating to nutrient deficiencies can be difficult to catch at first. Many factors may be the culprit, including temperature, pH, electrical errors, system leaks, or others. There could be toxic effects of some nutrients that contain irregular contents of salt or mineral concentrations, which affects the plant's growth. First, you'll need to identify the source of the problem, then you can find the strategies to help mitigate it.

Solution: Make a good mixture of your nutrient solution by measuring and diluting it to suit your plant species. For example, if there is too much salt in the solution, you can add some distilled water to dilute the salt. Another good method is to flush out the solution and replace it with a fresh solution. Often, keeping the water flowing can help lower the concentration of salt too. Monitoring the nutrient solution's pH and electrical conductivity can also help you detect any impurities present in the solution. Here are two more ways to avoid the presence of unwanted substances:

- Reverse osmosis: This is a process where impurities are forcefully passed through a semipermeable membrane to separate them from the water, thereby purifying it. The purified water can be used to mix the nutrient solutions for your system.
- Activated carbon filter: This method uses the help of granular activated carbon (GAC) to filter impurities out of water or solutions, especially in organic solutions. GAC filters help remove unwanted chemicals from water and reduce the presence of toxic substances.

14. Use of hard water:

Hard water is water that contains dissolved minerals or salts. Although hard water is not harmful to us, it is a problem when using it in your hydroponic system. Hard water contains minerals such as calcium and magnesium that mix with other nutrients in the solution, creating a problem for your plant's nutrient intake. You may not be aware of the amount of minerals that could be present if you use hard water often. When calcium compounds react in the water solution to form salts, plants will not be able to absorb the solution.

Solution: The first option is to dilute the solution with distilled water, which is water that is purified through boiling and condensation, or purified water such as what is obtained through reverse osmosis. Alternatively, you can use a purified water source to mix nutrient solutions, which will reduce the concentration of the minerals in the hard water and lower the effect on the nutrient solution concentration. You can measure the amount of total dissolved solids using a TDS meter to determine whether the concentration level is harmless or not. The lowest tolerable level would be 200 ppm, which may not cause a problem with the nutrient solution (Courtney, 2019a).

15. Plant diseases:

Plants grown in hydroponics are less susceptible to diseases than plants grown in soil, but hydroponic plants can still become infected with diseases. It's important to be diligent about regularly monitoring your plants' conditions and environment—including temperature, humidity, and lighting—so that the roots and other parts of the plants are as protected as possible from disease.

Solution: The best way to avoid and keep your plants free from pathogens or diseases caused by bacteria, viruses, or fungi is to keep the atmosphere around your garden unwelcoming to these intruders. Keep the temperature, humidity, and other factors under control by maintaining the conditions that prevent pathogens or diseases from occurring.

In order to achieve any goal, you'll have to overcome all the challenges that may get in your way. Preventing problems in as many ways as you can is the first step, but there are always ways to respond to any issue that comes up. Another way to do this is by putting your own ideas and knowledge into practice, so in the next chapter, we'll talk about how you can build your own hydroponic garden.

10

DIY SYSTEMS

" *All the flowers of all the tomorrows are in the seed of today.*

— CROFT M. PENTZ

Hydroponic systems offer many choices for gardeners, and as we know, there is a wide variety of hydroponic techniques to choose from. In addition to those, if you want to learn the ins and outs of a hydroponic system and have personal experience setting up your own customized system, you can create your own hydroponic setup. Building your own do-it-yourself, or DIY, system will help you understand how it all works as you learn about the details and components while assembling it.

BASIC HYDROPONIC DESIGNS AND HOW TO CHOOSE

Common hydroponic techniques used by many experienced gardeners have all been discussed previously, but I think they are worth mentioning again. There are two kinds of hydroponic systems: passive and active. Passive systems work without the help of air pumps, and active systems include the use of air pumps and other supporting equipment. The basic hydroponic systems that we have covered in this book are:

- Ebb and flow method
- Deep water culture (DWC)
- Wick system
- Nutrient film technique (NFT)
- Aeroponics
- Drip system
- Kratky method

When choosing which type of hydroponic system you are going to use, you'll want to have a good understanding of the whole system and how it works. Doing a little research can help you learn the pros and cons of each system type before going forward with the process. Once you've decided on the type of system you're going to use, gather all the equipment, supplies, and tools needed, particularly for an active system. For passive systems, you only need to worry about the water supply and nutrients. It's important to take all of the necessary steps to help your hydroponic garden run smoothly. There are many wholesale hydroponic supply stores either in your area or online that can provide the equipment and supplies you'll need to set up your hydroponic garden.

To get a better idea of the type of system you may want to build, take a look at the table below where I discuss some pros and cons of each type of hydroponic system.

Hydroponic system	Pros	Cons
Ebb and flow method (active)	• Efficiently uses water and electricity	• May create imbalance of wet and dry conditions for the plant if not controlled properly
Deep water culture (active)	• Low maintenance cost • Requires basic equipment • Recirculates water	• Suitable for growing short-period plants and medium or small plants only
Wick system (passive)	• Good for small plants • Easy to use • Low cost	• Not suitable for large plants
Nutrient film technique (active)	• Contains a film that helps roots perspire • Does not always require a growing medium	• Roots may grow to such a length that they start intertwining
Aeroponics (active)	• Roots receive enough oxygen • Roots can easily absorb water and don't often dry out • Easy maintenance	• Expensive compared to some techniques
Drip system (active)	• Plants receive a better and more controlled flow of nutrients • Can be used commercially	• Does not recirculate the water solution
Kratky method (passive)	• Simplest of all methods • Inexpensive • No equipment required • Adaptable	• Vulnerable to growth of algae or bacteria • Not suitable for all types of plants
Vertical system (active)	• Requires less space • Can grow crops year-round • Minimal use of pesticides	• Requires special equipment • Initial costs may be high • Limited varieties of crops

If you want to choose the most efficient and cost-effective system, the deep water culture system, wick system, or nutrient film technique would be the best choices, especially if you are a beginner. If you're looking for larger yields, you might consider the ebb and flow or aeroponic system.

HOW TO KEEP COSTS DOWN

Hydroponic systems have many options and may demand various resources in order for them to work correctly, but if you are looking for an inexpensive way to build your hydroponic system, there are options for that too. Hydroponic gardens do not have to consist of expensive equipment, fancy setups, and costly utilities. You can create one with inexpensive products and equipment to help lower your costs. For instance, deep water culture is one of the least expensive methods in hydroponics, and the system can be built from scratch. Here are some cost-effective ways you can install a deep water culture hydroponic garden:

Use recycled containers: You don't need to purchase hydroponic-specific containers from a fancy garden shop. You can use any large container lying around the house or garage as a reservoir. A plastic storage tub, children's wading pool, big bucket, or Styrofoam cooler can be used. If what you have on hand will work for your purposes and is clean and free of holes or cracks, you can use it!

Use inexpensive containers: Big buckets (5 gallons) and storage bins are items that work well as hydroponic reservoirs, and you can find them at any hardware or discount store. When choosing a bucket or bin, be sure to get one that is opaque and not transparent to avoid algae growth.

Make your own nutrient solution: If you're starting out with a smaller setup, it may make more sense for you to make your own nutrient solutions rather than buying them. For a basic hydroponic setup, you will need 2 tsp (10 mL) of fertilizer and 1 tsp (5 mL) of Epsom salt (magnesium sulfate) per gallon (3.8 L) of water. Epsom salt is available at pharmacies or grocery stores, while soluble fertilizers can be found at garden stores or online.

Make your own net pots: You can use food-grade plastic containers as net pots by adding some holes in the bottom to support your plant roots. Use a low-cost medium such as coco coir and place it in the pots to keep the plants upright. You can reuse the pots by simply sanitizing them.

Make use of sunlight: Sunlight is the first source of energy your plants need in their growing process, and you can get lots of it for no cost. Try to use the natural sunlight available to you as much as possible by placing your hydroponic system near a window or on the patio. If you still cannot find the right spot and your indoor plants need more light, you can use simple shop lights or fluorescent lights to provide light to your plants at a lower cost. In the case of larger plants, you will need proper fluorescent grow lights. I would not recommend fluorescent lights for all kinds of plants as they will not provide sufficient light. Full-spectrum LED lights are another inexpensive option.

As a beginner, it's best to start small and simple as you are learning how to garden in your hydroponic system. You only need to gather the basic resources, and this can be done by using everyday items you may already have at home. Go slow and steady, and soon you'll start to develop more ideas to improve your hydroponic garden.

DESIGN YOUR OWN SYSTEM

Hydroponic systems can be cumbersome and simple at the same time. If you are looking for a large yield of fruits and vegetables, you need a bigger space and more equipment for more than one system. If you want to make a simple and easy hydroponic system with minimal investment, you can design your own. One of the simplest and most efficient methods in hydroponics is the deep water culture (DWC) system as you only need a few resources to make it work, allowing you to grow clean, fresh, and nutritious food in your own home. This system is easy to manage, and once you understand it, you'll find it fascinating and want to continue growing plants this way. I gave you a broad idea of what the DWC system is earlier in the book, but I will explain it in more detail here.

For a deep water culture system, you will need the following things:

- A large container or 5-gal bucket
- Net pots (2–4 in.)
- An air pump and air stone (aquarium bubbler) of standard size, available at a gardening or aquarium store
- Liquid nutrients from a greenhouse store
- A pH meter
- A measuring cup
- A pipette
- A saw
- A drill

You want your 5-gal container to be deep enough so that the water has space and the nutrient solution will be stable. In shallow containers, this is more difficult, and you'll often have to add more water. As I mentioned earlier, you will want to use a nontransparent container that will not allow light to pass through as this can encourage the growth of algae. If you have trouble finding an opaque container, you can use a lighter one and wrap a black garbage bag around it to keep most light out.

Deep water culture buckets

You may already have many of these items lying around your home, but you can also find all these resources in any hardware or gardening store. You can learn more about any of these items by doing some extra research online about each item and its use. Once you have gathered your materials, you can follow these easy steps:

1. First, drill some holes in the container lid to place the net pots in to allow the plants to grow freely—make sure the holes are slightly smaller than the pots so they don't fall into the nutrient solution. As for the roots, the net pots help them create space to grow in the water. You can use a hole saw to make the holes in the lid; these can be found in any hardware store.

2. Next, connect an air pump to your container to ensure the oxygen level is good for your plants. Be sure to adjust the air pump so that it does not suck in water while it's operating. Some air pumps have a valve to check this, but not all. If your pump doesn't have one, keep it above the water level to be on the safe side. Finally, connect the air stone to the air pump with a tube to the valve. There should be an arrow to show you where they need to be connected. Place the air stone inside the water.

3. Place your container where you want to keep it, fill it with water, and add your nutrients. Using a measuring cup, take a measurement of 2 mL of the nutrient per 1 L of water. So if you have a 15-gallon (57 L) container, you'll add 114 mL of each nutrient to the water.

4. Adjust the pH of the water to suit each particular plant's needs. Since water has a pH of 6.5–7.5, you might have to adjust it with the help of an acid, like phosphoric acid, which is commercially used in hydroponics. There are easy-to-use kits with solutions to adjust the pH, and you may be able to find one for less than $30. You will need a pipette for measuring the right amount, or volume. Remember to use gloves when handling acids, and be sure to mix the solution well.

5. To start your hydroponic garden, turn on the air pump and place the air stone into the reservoir.

6. Place your plants with some medium-sized Rockwool plugs or hydroton clay pellets into the net pots. And now you are ready to go! If you want to use seeds instead of a starter plant, you can do that using the same Rockwool plugs, and they will germinate there too, but the best option is to germinate the seeds before planting them in the medium. A simpler process for germination is to place the seeds on a damp paper towel and put them on a tray with a cover. The seeds will sprout within one to two weeks.

As I've mentioned, it's good practice to monitor the pH throughout the plant's growing period and keep a record of your water solution composition. It's also useful to regularly check other parameters, such as TDS and EC.

Step-By-Step Design Solution

If you want to save money while getting your hydroponic system running, you should follow this step-by-step process. Because it's the easiest hydroponic system to use, we'll go through the steps for building your own deep water culture system in this section.

Step 1: Find a location

You know what they say—location, location, location! This is the first decision you'll make when setting up your hydroponic system, big or small. Once you have found the best position and space for your hydroponic garden, you can set it up there. Be sure to take its surroundings into consideration as well. Be sure to keep in mind access to water and power sources when choosing your location, especially for active systems such as the deep water culture system.

Step 2: Gather your materials

After determining where you'll place your hydroponic system, you'll want to gather everything you need to get it set up. Here are some of the basic supplies, tools, and equipment you'll need:

- opaque container with lid
- mesh pots or net pots
- your chosen medium
- nutrients
- air pump
- air stone
- razor knife
- pencil
- compass
- syringe

Step 3: Prepare the pots

Trace the shape of the pots you've chosen onto the lid of your container and make a hole to place the pots in. Make the size of the holes small enough so that the pots sit in them tightly.

Step 4: Set up the aeration equipment

Make another hole in the upper part of the container to allow the air stone connector to pass through and place the air stone in the container. Connect the air pump to the air stone.

Step 5: Sanitize the system

You want to make sure your container is clean and free of contaminants before adding your water and nutrients. To sanitize the container, fill it with water and add chlorine bleach. You can aerate the mixture with the air pump to circulate the bleach evenly. Once this is done, rinse and dry the container thoroughly.

Step 6: Add the nutrient solution

Once your hydroponic garden is in its permanent place, you can add the water and nutrients. A good general rule is to use 1 tsp (5 mL) of the nutrient for every 1 gal (3.8 L) of water. So if you're using 15 gal (56.8 L) of water, you'll add 15 tsp (75 mL) of nutrients (Trebuchet03, 2022). Keep your aeration pump on while adding the nutrients to the water to help everything thoroughly mix together.

Step 7: Prepare your plants

If you are using "starts" or seedlings you purchased from a nursery, you'll want to prepare them by washing off any excess dirt. Before placing your plants, you'll want to soak the medium in the nutrient solution to soften it. Once it's saturated, you'll place a little bit of the medium into the pots, then add the plants, and then add a little more of the medium on top to fully cover the roots. Once the pots are prepared, you're ready to place them in the holes you made in the container lid.

Step 8: Seeding (if needed)

When using a seed, you'll place it in the medium for it to germinate and into the pot that is placed in the lid of the container. You want to be careful with seeds as they start to germinate, and you can cover the pot to give it some extra protection. Note that if you are using Rockwool as your medium, you'll want to use Rockwool cubes for germinating seeds. Again, be sure to soak the medium before placing the seeds to soften the glass fiber contained in Rockwool, which could harm the seed.

Step 9: Maintenance

Maintaining your garden once it's up and running is just as important as setting it up properly in the first place. Because you built your system yourself, you can monitor every step and aspect of the process from germinating or placing seedlings to controlling the nutrient solution and checking the air pump. In larger hydroponic gardens, there are options for recycling or recirculating the nutrient solution and water, but in your case, you'll have to replace the nutrient solution yourself; you'll also have to refill the water when it gets low. In the beginning, you'll want to fill the container up to the bottom of the pots, but once the roots start growing, you won't have to fill it up as much. Check the air pump to ensure good air circulation and thorough mixing of the nutrient solution. Aeration also helps keep the roots from becoming soggy.

Step 10: Things to take care of

You can grow your hydroponic garden outdoors or indoors, but each one requires certain steps to help the garden be a success. Outdoors, you have plenty of sunlight, but you may need to install equipment and means for a proper water supply. Indoors, you'll generally have an easier time accessing water, but you will need to take steps to replace the sunlight that isn't as accessible to your plants inside. Grow lights are the best option for your indoor hydroponic setup, especially if you are in a region where daylight is limited at certain times of year.

You might need to think about how you'll drain water if it overflows and needs to be collected so it can be reused. One option is to install a valve system where the water can be controlled by draining it out or stopping the flow. There are different types of valves available, but some of the more common ones are gate valves and ball valves.

Last of all, check the pH, conductivity, and temperature of your water solution weekly. Local stores offer free testing if you can find one near you. In larger operations, this needs to be carried out on a regular basis.

Step 11: Pest control

We've talked about pests and control methods in earlier chapters, but I would like to add here that you can choose nontoxic methods of pest control and chemicals that will not harm you or the environment. Some of these nontoxic or organic methods use things such as

- neem oil
- garlic spray
- insects that feed on pests
- diatomaceous earth

Besides applying these harmless organic pesticides, you can help prevent pests from entering your garden with techniques such as cleaning and sanitizing your gardening tools and garden area, quarantining new plants, rotating crops, and maintaining the water quality.

Step 12: Lighting

Lighting is an essential part of your hydroponic system as it is needed especially for indoor gardens where daylight is limited. When setting up your indoor hydroponic garden, you will want to explore the various lighting options. Though there is a huge selection, you want to choose the type of lighting that will serve your purposes. As we've discussed, there are different kinds of bulbs you can use at different stages of your plants' growth cycles. The most common are T5, T12, and HID (MH or HPS). You can choose a certain kind of bulb for each growth stage and save a little bit of money by buying them one at a time rather than all at once. For example, you can use MH bulbs during the growing stage and change them out for HPS bulbs in the flowering or fruit stage of a plant.

Now that you know the steps to building your own hydroponic garden and will have yours up and running in no time, you'll want to make good use of the delicious produce you grow, which is what we'll talk about in the next chapter.

11

DELECTABLE, FRESH, AND DELICIOUS

Cooking demands attention, patience, and, above all, a respect for the gifts of the earth. It is a form of worship, a way of giving thanks.

— JUDITH B. JONES

Hydroponically growing plants—especially vegetables, leafy greens, and herbs—is not only a clean and cost-effective way to garden, but it also offers a reliable source of healthy food. There are so many recipes and ways to be innovative with the fresh, tasty produce you've grown. On a larger scale, hydroponic gardens have become popular among celebrities and chefs. Chefs love to use locally grown veggies in their dishes, and they last longer too. Professional chef Michael Anthony loves making his own "hydroponic" salad with butter lettuce that was grown locally and is fresh from the garden (Dupuis, 2022). Another benefit of hydroponic gardening is that you can grow any kind of produce all year long regardless of whether it's in season.

Vertical farming in hydroponics has proven to provide a reliable source of ingredients in vegetarian dishes that are nutritious and healthy. One company that grows vegetables and leafy greens using vertical farming on a larger scale is Eden Green Technology, and they are growing them with cost-efficient and energy-saving equipment (Dupuis, 2022).

TRUTH ABOUT HYDROPONICALLY GROWN CROPS

In today's gardening and farming world, hydroponics has taken a vital role. People have commended planting hydroponic vegetables and herbs, saying that they last longer in the refrigerator. Martha Stewart, a businesswoman, writer, and celebrity personality, has praised how fresh her hydroponically grown arugula has turned out (Dupuis, 2022).

There are several reasons that hydroponic vegetables and produce are in demand by many, including restaurants and supermarkets. Hydroponically grown produce can be altered with various practices and techniques, such as making changes to the nutrient solution, in order to make it more nutritious. Unlike other farming methods, you can control the garden conditions in hydroponic systems.

Here are some fun facts about hydroponic gardening:

- You can provide plants with an ideal spectrum of light by growing them indoors.
- You can adjust the light to grow your plants with better or larger leaves.
- Providing the maximum amount of water for each plant can enhance the taste of your hydroponic vegetables and fruits.

- You can eat your hydroponically grown vegetables fresh from your garden, eliminating the time it takes produce to get from a farm to the grocery store to your table, especially in vertical farming systems because the crops get more exposure to sunlight and air moisture and therefore grow even faster.
- You can manipulate the flavors of your hydroponic fruits and vegetables.

Tastes vary from person to person, and our tastes can change as we get older. A sweet, juicy strawberry may be bland and tasteless to an older person. Therefore, we may not be able to understand people's personal tastes all the time. Some people love very sweet flavors, while others prefer less sweetness in their food.

INTENSIFY YOUR FOOD FLAVOR

Another amazing aspect of hydroponic produce is the ability you have to manipulate the flavor of the food you are growing. We experience flavor through our senses of taste and smell. We perceive sweet, sour, bitter, and salty flavors when these senses work together. This is how we ultimately understand the flavor of any food. Volatile and aromatic compounds in fruits and vegetables provide their flavor and allow us to savor their taste. Good food is judged by taste, texture, and aroma, which can be influenced through your intentional practices in hydroponic gardening. In other words, we can alter the flavors of our vegetables, fruits, and herbs by simply changing certain parameters such as electrical conductivity, nutrients, or sunlight exposure. These are some ways you can change the flavor of your hydroponic produce to make it taste better:

Regulating sweetness: Sweetness in fruits and vegetables can be controlled by influencing the osmotic potential in the root zone of the plants. Osmotic potential is a process where water molecules move from one concentration to another due to a difference in salt or sugar molecules present. By reducing the water intake into the roots, you create a stress that will cause an alteration to the plant's flavors. This alteration will show a higher electrical conductivity in the solution due to moisture stress in the roots. This method is used in greenhouse gardens where the taste of tomatoes or fruits is improved. You can also use this technique with chili peppers and berries, though the impact on taste is not as great. This method can also be applied to herbs to increase their aroma and flavor.

Genetics: Genetics play a very important role in your garden's outcome. When you want to alter the taste and flavor of a plant, you can choose the genes that produce the best flavor in the cultivars you plant in your garden to ensure it grows the tastiest produce. This means you should choose the type of a certain plant that is genetically the most flavorful and delicious. For example, choose the best aromatic herbs that can be planted as cuttings or cultivars in your hydroponic garden to get the same results every time you plant them. While you do that, you can increase the electrical conductivity and adjust conditions such as the temperature, lighting, and humidity as well as the nutrient solution to enhance the flavor.

Light and temperature: Altering the lighting and temperature can also change the taste or aroma of your hydroponic fruits, vegetables, and herbs. For instance, you can boost the level of sugar in fruits, including tomatoes, by providing more light during the growing stage, which allows the roots to absorb more sugar (Johnson, 2018a). This is also possible in indoor hydroponic gardens where you can control your own lighting system by allowing extra light. Likewise, temperature can be controlled in a hydroponic system, and increasing the temperature will increase the production of food and sugar in the plants.

Increasing macronutrients: Boosting the amount of macronutrients, such as potassium or calcium, will enhance the taste of fruits and vegetables. Crops such as tomatoes can be altered in flavor with this method. Potassium is a vital source of flavor in many fruits and vegetables, and you can control this in your own garden.

Nutrient solution electrical conductivity: Altering the nutrient solution's EC is another way to improve the flavors of your crops. When you increase the EC, for instance by adding a mineral that changes the EC of your nutrient solution, you are producing a stress in the nutrient balance between the minerals in the solution and the minerals in the plant, and this causes a change in the taste and flavor; this is a great strategy to use with aromatic crops. The compounds, or content of minerals, become more concentrated, and this helps to enhance the flavor as well.

10 BEST RECIPES TO MAKE WITH YOUR HYDROPONICALLY GROWN VEGETABLES

Vegetables and leafy greens are some of the best produce to grow in your hydroponic garden. There are countless delicious recipes you can make to put your fresh produce to use. In this section, we'll look at 10 great recipes you can make using your hydroponic produce.

Arugula Pesto

Ingredients

- 1/4 c pine nuts, toasted
- 2 c arugula leaves
- 1/2 c Parmesan cheese, grated
- 1/2 c extra virgin olive oil
- 1/2 lemon for juice
- 1 clove garlic
- 1/2 tsp salt

Preparation

1. Blend pine nuts, arugula, Parmesan, lemon, garlic, olive oil, and salt in a food processor (Heidi, 2022).

Cold Cucumber Soup

Ingredients

- 2 1/4 lb cucumbers, cut in half and seeded
- 1 shallot, chopped
- 1 1/2 c Greek yogurt
- 2 tbsp tarragon leaves
- 1/3 c dill
- 1/4 c parsley leaves
- 1/4 c olive oil
- 1 garlic clove
- ground white pepper to taste
- salt to taste
- 1/2 lemon for juice

- 1/2 red onion, chopped

Preparation

1. Blend cucumbers, yogurt, olive oil, shallot, garlic, lemon juice, tarragon, parsley, dill, salt, and pepper until smooth.
2. Chill for at least 8 hours.
3. Serve with chopped red onion, diced cucumber, a sprinkle of salt and pepper, and a drizzle of olive oil on top (Zimmern, 2023).

Potato Chive Soup

Ingredients

- 5–6 peeled potatoes, diced
- 4 garlic cloves, minced
- 1 onion, chopped
- 1 c chives, chopped
- 3 c vegetable broth
- 1 tbsp dill, chopped
- 2 tbsp extra virgin olive oil
- 1 tsp dried thyme
- 1/2 tsp red pepper flakes (can be adjusted according to taste)
- 2 tsp salt
- 1 tsp pepper
- 2 c water

Preparation

1. Add olive oil to a heated soup pot on medium heat.
2. Add onions and a sprinkle of salt and pepper; sauté for 5 minutes.
3. Add chives, potatoes, and garlic; sauté for 4 minutes.
4. Add water, broth, thyme, dill, salt, pepper, and red pepper flakes; bring to boil.
5. Simmer on low heat for 20–25 minutes.
6. Use an immersion blender to blend the ingredients into a smooth liquid. If needed, add more broth or water to achieve desired consistency.
7. Serve topped with chives and seasoned with salt and pepper (Irene, 2015).

Italian Pasta Salad

Ingredients

- 1/2 lb pasta, uncooked
- 1/4 c red onion, chopped
- 1/2 red bell pepper, chopped
- 1/2 green bell pepper, chopped
- 1 1/2 c grape tomatoes
- 1/2 c black olives
- 3 oz salami
- 4 oz bocconcini mozzarella balls, cut in half
- 1 1/2 tbsp fresh parsley, chopped
- 3 tbsp extra virgin olive oil
- 1 1/2 tbsp lemon juice
- 1/2 c Italian dressing
- 1 tbsp Parmesan cheese

Preparation

1. Cook the pasta per package directions with salt to taste.
2. Rinse cooked pasta in cold water.
3. In a large bowl, add the rest of the ingredients, top with Italian dressing, and mix well.
4. Chill in the refrigerator for 2 hours.
5. Toss salad and sprinkle with Parmesan before serving (Hu, 2022b).

Greek Salad

Ingredients

- 3 c romaine lettuce, chopped
- 1 small red onion, chopped
- 1 medium green pepper, chopped
- 1 medium cucumber, quartered and sliced
- 1 c cherry or grape tomatoes
- 1/4 c crumbled Feta cheese
- 1/4 c Kalamata olives, whole

Dressing

- 1/2 tsp dried oregano
- 1 1/2 tbsp fresh lemon juice
- 1/4 tsp pepper
- 1/4 tsp salt
- 2 tbsp extra virgin olive oil

Preparation

1. Add lettuce, onion, green pepper, cucumber, tomatoes, Feta, and olives to a bowl.
2. In a separate bowl, mix salt, pepper, lemon juice, olive oil, and oregano well to make the dressing.
3. Pour dressing over salad and combine (Hu, 2021d).

Chicken Garden Salad With Ranch Dressing

Ingredients

- 1 chicken breast
- 1 head romaine lettuce, chopped
- 3 radishes, sliced
- 1 c grape tomatoes, cut in half
- 1 c purple cabbage, chopped
- 1 mini cucumber, sliced
- 1/4 red onion, sliced
- 1 medium carrot, shaved
- 1/4 c ranch dressing
- 1/2 c croutons
- 1 tbsp vegetable oil

Preparation

1. Season chicken breast with salt and pepper to taste on both sides.
2. Heat oil in a pan and cook chicken breast thoroughly, about 4–7 minutes on each side. Set aside to cool.
3. Add all remaining ingredients except ranch dressing and croutons in a bowl and toss.

4. Slice chicken and add to bowl, tossing again.
5. Top with ranch dressing and croutons (Hu, 2021c).

Coleslaw

Ingredients

- 2 c purple cabbage
- 3 c green cabbage or broccoli stems
- 1 c carrots
- 1/2 c mayonnaise
- 1/2 tbsp apple cider vinegar
- 1 tbsp vinegar or lemon juice
- 1/2 tsp celery seeds
- 1/2 tsp sugar
- salt and pepper to taste

Preparation

1. Shred cabbage and carrots finely and combine in a large bowl.
2. In a separate smaller bowl, mix together celery seeds, both vinegars, mayonnaise, sugar, salt, and pepper.
3. Add the contents of the small bowl to the large bowl and mix to combine all ingredients.
4. You can chill for 1 hour or serve immediately (Hu, 2022c).

Caesar Salad

Ingredients

- 2 heads romaine lettuce, chopped
- 1 c Caesar dressing
- 1/2 c Parmesan cheese, grated
- 1–2 c croutons

Preparation

1. Toss lettuce, Parmesan cheese, and croutons in a bowl.
2. Drizzle with dressing and toss again (Hu, 2022a).

Grilled Shrimp Salad

Ingredients

- 1 lb large deveined shrimp, peeled and tails removed
- 5–6 c mixed greens
- 1/2 red onion, sliced
- 1 red bell pepper, sliced
- 1 avocado, sliced
- 2 tbsp garlic, minced
- 2 tbsp lemon juice
- 2 tbsp olive oil
- 1/2 tbsp Italian seasoning
- 1 tsp paprika
- 3/4 tsp black pepper
- 1 1/2 tsp salt
- Skewers

Dressing

- 2 tbsp olive oil
- 1 tbsp lemon juice
- 1 tsp black pepper
- 1 tsp salt

Preparation

1. In a zip-lock bag, add shrimp, garlic, paprika, Italian seasoning, 1/2 tsp pepper, 1 tsp salt, 1 tbsp lemon juice, and 1 tbsp olive oil. Shake the bag to coat evenly. You can also toss ingredients in a bowl. Allow to marinate for at least 15 minutes.
2. Place 4–5 seasoned shrimp on a skewer.
3. Heat a pan with oil and grill each skewer for about 3–4 minutes on each side.
4. In a separate large bowl, combine onion, bell pepper, avocado, and mixed greens. Remove shrimp from skewers and add to salad.
5. In a small bowl, mix 1 tbsp lemon juice, 1 tbsp olive oil, 1/4 tsp of pepper, and 1/2 tsp of salt to make the dressing. You can also use a bottled oil-based dressing instead.
6. Top salad with dressing and toss once more (Hu, 2021b).

Caprese Salad

Ingredients

- 1 c bocconcini mozzarella balls, cut in half
- 2 c cherry tomatoes, cut in half
- 1/4 c fresh basil, chopped

- 1 tbsp balsamic vinegar
- 2 tbsp olive oil
- 1/4 tsp dried oregano
- 1/4 tsp black pepper
- 1/2 tsp salt

Preparation

1. Combine mozzarella balls, basil, and tomatoes in a bowl.
2. In a separate bowl, mix balsamic vinegar, olive oil, salt, pepper, and oregano.
3. Pour seasoning mixture over salad ingredients and toss to combine (Hu, 2021a).

VEGGIE TREATS

In this section, you'll find more delicious recipes for you to put your fresh, homegrown hydroponic produce to use! From quick snacks to delectable entrées, there are so many ways to create healthy and tasty dishes with your hydroponic vegetables.

Grilled Radishes

Ingredients

- 4 c round radishes, cut in half
- 1 tsp fresh thyme, chopped
- 2 tbsp butter, melted and browned
- salt to taste

Preparation

1. Warm up your grill or pan and coat radish halves with some cooking oil. Flat side down, place radishes in pan or on grill.
2. Grill radishes for 3–4 minutes on each side.
3. Place in a serving bowl or dish and top with butter, thyme, and salt (Danae, 2021).

Garlic Kale

Ingredients

- 2 bunches of kale leaves, thinly sliced
- 3 garlic cloves, sliced
- 3 tbsp extra virgin olive oil
- 1/4 tsp red chili flakes
- salt and pepper to taste

Preparation

1. Heat oil in a large skillet and add garlic and chili flakes. Sauté for 2 minutes.
2. Add kale in increments and toss to distribute the oil.
3. Cover the skillet and let it steam for 5 minutes.
4. Season with salt and pepper and cook until there is no moisture left (Farris, 2023).

Spinach Bake

Ingredients

- 3 3/4 c frozen spinach
- 2–3 garlic cloves, minced
- 1/4 c shallots, chopped
- 3/4 c cream cheese, softened
- 2 tbsp Parmesan cheese, grated
- 2 tbsp breadcrumbs
- 2 tbsp unsalted butter
- 1/4 tsp red pepper flakes
- 1 tsp salt
- 1 tsp black pepper

Preparation

1. Preheat your oven to 375 °F (190 °C).
2. Thaw the spinach and use a paper towel to soak up as much moisture as possible.
3. Add butter to a saucepan and sauté shallots at medium heat for 3–5 minutes.
4. Add garlic and stir a few times.
5. Add the spinach, red pepper flakes, cream cheese, salt, and pepper and mix well.
6. Pour mixture into a baking dish and top with Parmesan and breadcrumbs.
7. Bake in the oven for 10–15 minutes until golden brown (Dozier, 2023).

Green Beans

Ingredients

- 1 lb fresh green beans, trimmed and cut in half
- 2 garlic cloves, minced
- 3 tbsp butter
- 1/8 tsp lemon pepper seasoning
- salt to taste

Preparation

1. Place the beans in a skillet and fill with water to cover beans. Bring to a boil.
2. Lower heat and simmer for 3–5 minutes, then drain water from skillet.
3. Stir in the butter for 1–2 minutes until melted. Add garlic and stir for another 1–2 minutes.
4. Season with salt and lemon pepper (LookWhatsCooking, 2023).

Grilled Sweet Pepper Soup

Ingredients

- 1 yellow onion
- 5 sun-dried tomatoes
- 6 red pointed or bell peppers, chopped
- 4 garlic cloves, whole
- 2 1/2 c vegetable stock
- 1/2 tbsp lemon juice
- 1 tbsp olive oil

- 1–2 tbsp crème fraîche
- 1–2 tbsp pesto sauce
- salt and pepper to taste

Preparation

1. Preheat your oven to 400 °F (205 °C).
2. Place garlic and pointed or bell peppers on a baking sheet. Drizzle olive oil and season with salt and pepper.
3. Roast in the oven for about 40 minutes.
4. Chop the onion and sauté in a large pan with olive oil.
5. Once onions have softened, add roasted garlic and peppers, sun-dried tomatoes, and vegetable stock to pan.
6. Simmer on low heat for 10 minutes.
7. Blend all ingredients with an immersion blender.
8. Add lemon juice and mix well.
9. Top with crème fraîche and pesto (Emily, 2020).

Green Frittata

Ingredients

- 2 c baby spinach
- 1 c fresh flat-leaf parsley leaves
- 1 c fresh basil leaves
- 1 1/2 c baby kale
- 4 asparagus stalks, shaved into strips
- 1 onion, sliced
- 1 zucchini, shaved
- 6 eggs
- 2 garlic cloves, crushed
- 1/4 c Parmesan cheese

- 2 1/4 c ricotta cheese
- 2 tbsp extra virgin olive oil
- 1–2 tsp lemon juice
- salt and pepper to taste

Preparation

1. Preheat your oven to 355 °F (180 °C).
2. Chop spinach and herbs in a food processor; blend until smooth.
3. Add eggs, Parmesan, and ricotta and season with salt and pepper; blend again until smooth.
4. Warm a pan with olive oil at medium heat and add onions; cook for 2–3 minutes.
5. Add garlic to pan with onions and stir, then add zucchini and kale.
6. Remove the pan from the heat and stir in the blended mixture.
7. Place the pan into the oven and cook for 20–25 minutes until golden and puffed.
8. Take out the pan and set it aside to cool for a few minutes.
9. Top with kale, asparagus, and a drizzle of olive oil and lemon juice (Quinn, 2016).

Spicy Eggplant Fritters

Ingredients

- 2 eggplants, sliced into half-inch circles
- 2 eggs
- 1 c Greek yogurt
- 1/2 c flour

- 1 c red-veined sorrel leaves
- 1 garlic clove, crushed
- 2 green onions, sliced
- 2 c panko breadcrumbs
- 1 lemon for juice
- 4 heirloom tomatoes, sliced
- 1 pomegranate, just for seeds
- 1 tsp sumac
- 1 tbsp extra virgin olive oil

Preparation

1. Set a colander on top of a bowl and place eggplant slices in the colander. Sprinkle with salt and set aside for 30 minutes. After 30 minutes, rinse with cool water and pat dry.
2. In a bowl, combine sumac and flour.
3. In a separate bowl, whisk eggs.
4. Place the breadcrumbs in another separate bowl.
5. Dip eggplant slices into flour mixture, then the eggs. Allow any excess egg to drip off, then dip in breadcrumbs, coating the entire slice of eggplant.
6. Heat olive oil in a frying pan. Cook eggplant slices in groups for 5–6 minutes on each side.
7. Mix garlic, lemon juice, and yogurt in a separate bowl then spread evenly on a serving platter.
8. Place eggplant fritters on top of yogurt mixture, and top with sorrel, green onion, tomato slices, and pomegranate seeds (Wood, 2017).

No-Meat Broccolini Balls

Ingredients

- 2 bunches of broccolini, chopped
- 1 onion, chopped
- 2 zucchini, shredded
- 2/3 c arugula leaves
- 3 garlic cloves, chopped
- 1 c oat bran
- 1 bunch marjoram with leaves removed
- 1/4 c psyllium husk
- 7/8 c goat's Feta
- 2 eggs
- 1/4 c olive oil
- 1 lemon for zest
- 1 tbsp lemon juice
- labneh, wrap bread, and sprouts for serving

Preparation

1. Chop the arugula, broccolini, and half the marjoram finely in a processor.
2. Add oat bran and psyllium husk to the mixture and combine.
3. Heat a frying pan with 1 tbsp olive oil and cook garlic and onion until soft, about 3–4 minutes.
4. Add the broccolini mix to the pan and stir for 1 minute, then set aside to cool.
5. After cooling, put eggs, lemon zest, and Feta in a bowl and combine with broccolini mix.

6. Use 2 tbsp of the mixture to make balls; should make around 22 balls.
7. Flatten the broccolini balls slightly and place them on a baking pan.
8. Heat some oil and cook the balls in a frying pan at medium–low heat for 2–3 minutes on each side for each batch of balls.
9. Add the zucchini, some oil, lemon juice, and the rest of the marjoram to a bowl to make a salad.
10. Serve the broccolini balls with the salad, labneh, wrap bread, and sprouts (Parish, 2016).

Vegetable Lasagna

Ingredients

- 1/2 butternut squash, peeled, deseeded, and cut in half
- 4 yellow squash
- 7/8 c peas, blanched
- 1/2 bunch basil leaves, torn
- 4 baby zucchini, flowers attached
- 2 c ricotta cheese
- 2 c Parmesan cheese, grated
- 3/4 c roasted almonds, chopped
- 1 lemon for zest and juice
- 1 tsp dried chili flakes
- 2 tbsp honey
- 1 tbsp apple cider vinegar
- 2 tbsp extra virgin olive oil

Preparation

1. Preheat the oven to 395 °F (200 °C).
2. Blend the Parmesan, ricotta, basil, peas, chili flakes, and lemon zest in a food processor.
3. Pour mixture into a bowl and mix in 1/2 cup almonds.
4. Place in the fridge to chill, covered.
5. Make a sauce with 1 tbsp of honey and 1 tbsp oil in a bowl.
6. Slice the butternut squash into quarter-inch-thick slices, microwave for 3 minutes, and then brush the sauce over it.
7. Layer the butternut squash slices in an 8 1/2-inch baking dish and top with 1/3 of the ricotta. Repeat with remaining butternut squash slices and ricotta to make two more layers.
8. Bake in the oven for 35 minutes. Allow to cool for a couple of minutes.
9. Slice the remaining squash and zucchini thinly, removing petals from the zucchini.
10. Make another sauce with lemon juice, apple cider vinegar, and remaining honey and olive oil in a bowl.
11. Top lasagna with the sliced zucchini, squash, and zucchini flowers and drizzle the vinegar, lemon, and honey sauce all over (Harley, 2016).

Grilled Romaine Lettuce

Ingredients

- 3–4 romaine hearts
- 2 tsp fresh herbs (oregano, thyme, or rosemary), chopped
- 3 tbsp extra virgin olive oil
- 1 tbsp red wine or cider vinegar

- 1/4 tsp salt
- 1/4 tsp black pepper

Preparation

1. Slice off the brown part of the bottom of the stem of the romaine hearts and remove any old leaves, but keep the leaves together with the stem.
2. Heat up your grill.
3. Mix salt, pepper, vinegar, and herbs in a bowl.
4. Brush the herb mixture over all the lettuce leaves.
5. Grill the lettuce, turning every minute or so, until all sides have browned.
6. Serve whole or chop them up for a salad. (Bauer, 2023).

FRUITY DELIGHTS

You can make some amazing desserts with your hydroponic fruits, so in this section, I've shared some yummy and flavorful recipes for sweet treats that feature strawberries and blueberries. Choose any one of these and surprise your loved ones with delicious fruity desserts.

Strawberry Mousse

Ingredients

- 2 c strawberries
- 1 1/4 c double cream
- 1/2 c baker's sugar

Preparation

1. Set 4 good strawberries aside for later. Chop the rest then blend in a food processor with the baker's sugar until smooth.
2. Set aside 4 tbsp of the strawberry puree.
3. Whisk the double cream in a bowl and fold in the strawberry puree until pink to prepare the mousse.
4. Place the puree you have set aside in 4 small glasses and use a spoon to top with mousse. Chill for 1 hour.
5. Cut the remaining strawberries in half and use them to garnish the mousse (Desmazery, n.d.).

Strawberry Lemonade

Ingredients

- 2 c strawberries, cut into quarters, plus whole strawberries for serving
- 7/8 c sugar
- 4–5 lemons, freshly squeezed
- 4 1/4 c water
- ice

Preparation

1. Put water and sugar in a saucepan and heat until sugar dissolves completely.
2. Set the pan aside to cool.
3. Place the strawberries in a food processor and blend until smooth.

4. Put the sugar water and strawberry puree in a pitcher and add lemon juice.

5. Stir to mix well and pour in glasses full of ice. Garnish with whole strawberries if you want (Goldsmith, n.d.).

Strawberry Ice Cream

Ingredients

- 2 c strawberries
- 5 egg yolks
- 2/3 c baker's sugar
- 1 1/4 c whole milk
- 2 1/2 c double cream
- 1–2 tsp lemon juice
- 2 tsp vanilla extract

Preparation

1. Blend the strawberries and lemon juice in a food processor.

2. Heat the milk and cream in a pan on medium heat until the mixture is warm.

3. Whisk egg yolks and sugar in a bowl for 1–2 minutes then add to the milk and cream mixture. Whisk as you combine.

4. Using a sieve, strain this into the pan and cook on low–medium heat until it thickens to form a custard.

5. Transfer the milk and egg yolk mixture to a bowl; cover and allow to cool for 10 minutes, then chill in the fridge for 1 hour.

6. Stir the vanilla and strawberry puree into the cold custard.

7. Freeze the ice cream in the freezer for 4 hours. While freezing, periodically whisk the ice cream or blend in a food processor to avoid the formation of crystals (Best, n.d.).

Apple and Blueberry Bread and Butter Crumble

Ingredients

- 2 3/4 c frozen blueberries, thawed
- 6 Granny Smith apples, peeled, cored, and cubed
- 1/4 c baker's sugar
- 1 tsp vanilla extract
- 2 tbsp brown sugar
- 1/4 c unsalted butter, chilled and chopped
- 1/3 c unsalted roasted peanuts, whole; 2 tbsp chopped
- 1/3 c whole almonds, roasted
- 1/4 c flaked almonds
- 2 tbsp flour
- 1/2 c whole-wheat flour
- icing and thin cream for serving

Preparation

1. Preheat your oven to 355 °F (180 °C).

For crumble:

a. Mix butter and both flours in a food processor until it looks like fine breadcrumbs, about 1 minute.
b. Add brown sugar and pulse to mix. (You can add 1–2 more tbsp of whole-wheat flour if mixture looks clumpy).

c. Add 1/3 c peanuts and whole almonds; pulse until roughly chopped, then set aside.

2. In a separate bowl, combine baker's sugar, vanilla, blueberries, and apples; mix well.
3. Pour fruit mixture into a 6 1/4 x 10 1/2-inch baking dish and top with an even layer of the crumble mixture.
4. Top with 2 tbsp chopped peanuts and flaked almonds.
5. Bake 45–50 minutes until bubbling and golden.
6. Top with icing and serve with thin cream (Quinn Davies, 2015).

Finnish Blueberry Pies

Ingredients

- 3/4 c baker's sugar
- 2 c flour
- 1 tsp baking powder
- 2 eggs
- 1/2 c unsalted butter, softened
- 1/2 c Greek yogurt
- 1/2 c crème fraîche
- 1 tsp vanilla bean paste
- 2 c blueberries, frozen

Preparation

1. Preheat the oven to 355 °F (180 °C).
2. Mix the sugar and butter in a stand mixer and beat for 3–4 minutes until creamy.
3. Add one egg and beat again.

4. Mix in baking powder and flour.
5. Take the dough and make eight divisions. Press each section into a lightly greased tart pan, pressing sides and bottom. Set aside.
6. Separately, mix egg, yogurt, crème fraîche, vanilla, and sugar; whisk until smooth.
7. Pour yogurt mixture evenly into each tart pan and top with 1/4 c blueberries.
8. Place tart pans on a tray and bake for 25–30 minutes until custard is set and topping is golden brown. Cool before serving (Esdaile, 2021).

HOSTING A PARTY!

Hosting a party can be fun and enlightening at the same time. You can get great ideas for a themed party with your hydroponic fruits and vegetables. Themed parties can incorporate food, and you can even do food-related activities at the party! Some great themes that incorporate your hydroponic produce are nature and Earth Day. This is a great way to show off your hydroponic fruits and vegetables and help others learn all while having fun.

Nature-Themed Party

These are some cute and easy-to-make foods you can serve at a nature-themed party—or any party!

1. Tomato egg mushroom

Ingredients: Cherry tomatoes, hard-boiled eggs, and cream cheese

Preparation: Arrange the eggs on a plate. Cut tomatoes in half and scoop out the inside. Place the half-tomatoes over the eggs so that it looks like a mushroom. Use cheese to make little dots on the tomatoes.

   2. Mashed potato snails

Ingredients: Chicken strips or hot dogs, boiled potatoes for mashed potatoes, carrots for garnish, peas, cucumber slices, and cheese (cubes or shredded)

Preparation: First, make some mashed potatoes with butter, salt, pepper, and milk and cook the hot dogs or chicken strips. Place a hot dog or chicken strip on a plate in a curved position (you can use toothpicks to hold it in place if needed) and place a mound of mashed potatoes directly on top of it to make it look like a snail. Make the antennae with some cucumber peels and garnish the bottom with carrots, peas, and cheese to look like the ground or grass.

Earth Day-Themed Party

Earth Day can be celebrated with a themed party that includes all the eco-friendly items and recipes you can think of. Get together with your friends or invite your kids' friends over and share your ideas, and you will find some fun activities to do. Here are some suggestions to get you started.

- **Decorations:** There are several items you can use as Earth Day decorations such as plants, aquariums, and images of nature. Get your family to help you draw and make pictures of beautiful flowers, butterflies, trees, and animals. Anything that has a naturey feel can be used to create a fun, Earth Day-worthy atmosphere for your party.

- **Green table:** Decorate a table with organic materials, a green tablecloth and place mats, and some LED candles. Use hydroponically grown ingredients to make a beautiful centerpiece. Terra-cotta pots and dishes are great options for your green table and bring an earthy vibe. You can also make use of recycled items such as brown craft paper or cardboard.

- **Plastic-free dinnerware:** Avoid plastic tableware that is a source of chemical pollution and use paper items that are readily available at any craft shop. You can use ceramic, clay, or bamboo dinnerware as well.

- **Organic drinks and meals:** Make your drinks from healthy fruits and vegetables such as lemon juice, cucumber, or mint. Your meals can include pea soup, pasta with broccoli or asparagus, and salads of different kinds garnished with cheese and croutons.

- **Eco-friendly gifts:** Giving gifts can be a fun way to express the spirit of Earth Day. You can present your guests with tokens of nature such as tiny pots of honey, plant seed packets, a miniature plant to keep in their homes, or even books on nature. These gifts should remind everyone of the importance of conserving nature and keeping it from being harmed. The gifts should help your guests understand how we can keep our Earth beautiful and clean by protecting natural resources.

Food Tasting

You can make your parties more fun by adding some tasting events as part of the festivities. You can include different dishes made up of ingredients that mainly come from your hydroponic garden as a way to introduce your homegrown fruits and vegetables. You can add various other items to pair with your hydroponic goodies, such as cheese, crackers, cream, or honey. Let your guests get some exciting tasting experiences that might inspire them to try their hand at hydroponic gardening. You can arrange your food selections on a decorative buffet, make different sorts of canapés, or even have blindfolded guessing games with your food. Kids will definitely enjoy this, especially if you have some delicious desserts made, such as the recipes listed in the previous section. Everyone can play these games and guess what ingredients are in the food as they taste each dish. You can even reward everyone with a gift that was also grown naturally in your garden or handcrafted by you such as flower arrangements or beautiful cards.

Celebration of the Earth

Earth Day is a day to celebrate our planet with numerous activities, campaigns, or programs with your friends, neighbors, and family. There are a number of things you can do to celebrate this day and continue practicing throughout the year. Taking care of the Earth and living sustainably is the goal of celebrating Earth Day. You can start by planting herbs and other hydroponic plants with your family to enjoy and learn about nature while practicing sustainable gardening at the same time. Discuss what kinds of plants are beneficial to nature and your local environment. You can also talk to friends or share posts on social media about the natural environment and topics related to sustainable agriculture.

Cleaning the neighborhood or a local park to remove trash, plastics, and other items that are harmful to the environment can be a great way to celebrate and contribute to positive change. On Earth Day and every day, you can try to use cleaner technologies and gardening methods that are good for the environment. Get rid of chemicals, pesticides, and harmful substances around your home and garden. You can practice organic methods for planting and applying fertilizers to your crops and plants. Here are some more ways you can celebrate Earth Day:

- **Conserve water:** Use water efficiently and recycle used water for tasks like watering plants and washing the car. Try not to keep the taps running when not in use.
- **Plant trees:** Plant some hydroponic herbs, vegetables, fruits, and flowers in your garden, and mark the occasion by planting a special symbolic tree in your yard. It will remind you every day throughout the year to continue the trend with your family.
- **Keep your garden free of chemicals:** Avoid using chemical pesticides and fertilizers in your garden. Make an effort to use natural methods or fertilizers that are safe for the environment when treating your plants.
- **Use nature-friendly resources:** Use organic fertilizers and alternative sources to supplement nutrients such as calcium, phosphates, nitrates, zinc, iron, and magnesium.
- **Practice the three Rs:** Incorporate the motto "reduce, reuse, recycle" as much as possible into your daily life. Try to recycle and repurpose as many items as you can. You can even do activities or arts and crafts projects with your kids using recycled items from your home and garden and display them on Earth Day.

- **Promote hydroponic gardening:** There are hydroponic systems where nutrients and water are recycled by pumps installed throughout the entire setup so no water or nutrients are wasted. You can also promote these concepts by putting up posters or banners or even giving presentations to bring attention to this eco-friendly technique. One good way to promote hydroponics is by displaying plants or flowers outside your home with labels so passersby can see them.

YOUR CHANCE TO HELP OTHERS
TAKE THE REINS OF THEIR HEALTH

Don't you wish everyone knew the pride and excitement that swell in your heart whenever you pick a juicy tomato, fresh herbs, or pretty flowers from your own hydroponic garden?

Now you know you can grow your own green oasis quickly and inexpensively… even if you live in an urban area or have a small garden.

Thank you so much for your support. I wish you many abundant harvests. Imagine how fulfilling it will be to transition from relying fully on store-bought goods to tucking into a feast made with colorful produce grown with your own two hands.

CONCLUSION

❝ *He that plants trees loves others besides himself.*

— THOMAS FULLER

Hydroponics is the new trend of gardening and will hopefully grow and expand even more in future generations. It is considered the future of farming because it incorporates new and efficient techniques that are very different from traditional agricultural practices that use soil as the sole nutrient provider (Boylan, 2020). We need to promote this technique of growing fruits, vegetables, and herbs organically with only water and nutrients. It is by far the most cost-effective method as it requires only a supply of water, nutrients, and light, whether through natural sunlight or the use of artificial lighting. It is not only an easy way to grow fresh food and beautiful plants, but it's also something you can enjoy with your family and share with friends and neighbors. There is simply no cleaner or healthier gardening technique than hydroponic gardening, and as you've learned in the pages of this book, there are so many ways to incorporate hydroponic gardening into your lifestyle and home and make it work with the resources and space you have available. You've also learned about the resources, materials, and environmental conditions needed to have a successful hydroponic garden all your own indoors, outdoors, or in a greenhouse.

Through this journey, we've also discussed how to prepare yourself and your space to install and even build your own hydroponic garden. The key is to start small and learn the tricks and strategies that will help you be successful with your hydroponic setup and grow your operation from there. You can start with the easier methods like the Kratky method or deep water culture system as a DIY project and eventually build your own greenhouse right beside your home if you want! Just follow the steps and tips given in this book and take it slow as you learn the ins and outs of hydroponic gardening. There are many products and supporting materials available on the internet and in gardening stores that will help you with anything you need, especially measuring instruments for TDS, EC, and pH. For DIY systems, you may not need to invest too much money right away because you can build them from scratch using items you may have lying around your home or that can be found for a low cost.

The benefits of hydroponic gardening are numerous, and this technique can be the solution to the loss of resources we are experiencing worldwide and provide an alternative to traditional farming. In the past, poor irrigation practices and agricultural techniques have caused a scarcity of our natural resources. According to the World Wildlife Fund (WWF), the percentage of decrease in invertebrate species has been increasing due to human exploitation for more industrial production (Boylan, 2020). It's vital that we find ways to generate renewable resources and reduce human interference with the environment and wildlife habitats. The unlimited demand for resources and overuse of land need to be curbed, and alternative agricultural methods are the only way to do this.

Hydroponics is a controlled farming technique, which means you can control the growth and conditions of your garden from the very beginning, starting with seedlings all the way through harvesting your yield. You have many natural and organic options for fighting diseases or pests.

There are many examples of people taking up hydroponic gardening in their homes and greenhouses and even turning it into a business to support themselves financially. Regina and Joe Villari have their own story of success with hydroponic gardening and how they started from a small operation to becoming owners of two companies, Villari Vineyards and Fresh Water Greens (Evan, 2015). Their farming experiences started 100 years ago when the siblings' grandfather came to the United States and grew fruits and vegetables and set up a vineyard on the same land. This practice was kept up by the family, and today Regina and Joe have vertical farming projects and a hydroponic greenhouse that mainly uses the nutrient film technique. This system has proven to be most efficient for them because it saves large amounts of water as the nutrient solution is recycled with the use of pumps. They grow herbs, lettuce, and other crops with an ecologically friendly approach 365 days a year and are able to maintain the highest standards.

We can follow Joe and Regina's lead and start planning our own hydroponic systems. Because of the numerous options for systems and setups, space is not a huge limiting factor, and you can embark on a new journey while beginning to live more sustainably. We have a duty to live more sustainably and economically. Once you've got the basics down and are diligent about managing your system, hydroponics offers a way to have access to fresh, clean produce no matter where you live or what time of year it is.

Think sustainably. Think clean. Help our environment!

Thank you so much for taking the first step to learn about hydroponic gardening by reading this book. I hope you've been inspired and gained the necessary knowledge to start your own hydroponic garden, and if you have, please consider leaving a review so others can begin their hydroponic journey as well.

REFERENCES

Adriana. (2023, January 12). *Easy home hydroponic set up*. Backyard Garden Lover. https://www.backyardgardenlover.com/home-hydroponics/

The Advanced Nutrients Team. (2014, March 24). *The four most common errors hydroponics growers make*. Advanced Nutrients. https://www.advancednutrients.com/articles/the-four-most-common-errors-hydroponic-growers-make/

The Advanced Nutrients Team. (2016, December 2). *How Advanced Nutrients pH Perfect® technology makes growing hydroponically brain-dead simpleTM!* Advanced Nutrients. https://www.advancednutrients.com/articles/ph-perfect-technology/

The Advanced Nutrients Team. (2022, September 20). *How to build your own hydroponics grow room—Calculating lighting & insulation needs (part 2)*. Advanced Nutrients. https://www.advancednutrients.com/articles/grow-room-calculating-lighting-insulation-needs/

Baron, K. (2021, February 21). *Put your basement to good use—start a hydroponic garden*. HappySprout. https://www.happysprout.com/inspiration/basement-hydroponic-garden/

Bauer, E. (2023, March 24). *Grilled romaine lettuce*. Simply Recipes. https://www.simplyrecipes.com/recipes/grilled_romaine_lettuce/

Best, C. (n.d.). *Strawberry ice cream*. BBC Good Food. https://www.bbcgoodfood.com/recipes/strawberry-ice-cream

Bowens, S. (n.d.). *All about marjoram*. A Pinch Of... http://www.apinchof.com/marjoram1013.html

Boylan, C. (2020, November 9). *The future of farming: Hydroponics*. PSCI. https://psci.princeton.edu/tips/2020/11/9/the-future-of-farming-hydroponics

Boyle, D. (n.d.). *Danny Boyle quotes*. BrainyQuote. https://www.brainyquote.com/quotes/danny_boyle_438501

Brahlek, A. (2023, January 16). *Advantages & disadvantages of hydroponics*. Trees.com. https://www.trees.com/gardening-and-landscaping/advantages-disadvantages-of-hydroponics

Bulla, A. (2022, April 6). *10 stunning flowers to grow hydroponically*. Gardening Chores. https://www.gardeningchores.com/hydroponic-flowers/

Buscaglia, L. (n.d.) *Leo Buscaglia quotes*. BrainyQuote. https://www.brainyquote.com/quotes/leo_buscaglia_121375#:

Chartier, L. (2021, February 11). *Hydroponics & nutrient application*. Greenhouse

Product News. https://gpnmag.com/article/hydroponics-nutrient-application/

Chris. (2021, January 17). *Beginner's guide to hydroponic systems.* Happy Hydro Farm. https://happyhydrofarm.com/guide-to-hydroponic-systems/

Coleridge, S. T. (2023, September 14). *The rime of the ancient mariner (text of 1834).* Poetry Foundation. https://www.poetryfoundation.org/poems/43997/the-rime-of-the-ancient-mariner-text-of-1834

Courtney, A. (2019a, September 26). 15 common problems with hydroponics and how to fix them. *Smart Garden Guide.* https://smartgardenguide.com/prob lems-with-hydroponics/

Courtney, A. (2019b, September 26). What is the best pH for hydroponics? *Smart Garden Guide.* https://smartgardenguide.com/best-ph-for-hydroponics/

Currey, C. J. (2017, April). *An introduction to pests in hydroponic production.* Produce Grower. https://www.producegrower.com/article/an-introduction-to-pests-in-hydroponic-production/

Danae. (2021, August 21). *Grilled radishes with brown butter, thyme and sea salt.* Recipe Runner. https://reciperunner.com/grilled-radishes-brown-butter-thyme-sea-salt/

D'Anna, C. (2022, August 31). *The basics of hydroponic lighting.* The Spruce. https://www.thespruce.com/hydroponic-lighting-basics-1939224

Deering, S. (2019, February 28). *Nature's 9 most powerful medicinal plants and the science behind them.* Healthline. https://www.healthline.com/health/most-powerful-medicinal-plants#gingko

Desmazery, B. (n.d.). *Easy strawberry mousse.* BBC Good Food. https://www.bbcgoodfood.com/recipes/easy-strawberry-mousse

Dozier, N. (2023, July 30). *Creamy spinach bake.* The Kitchn. https://www.thek itchn.com/recipe-creamy-spinach-bake-recipes-from-the-kitchn-215729

Dr. Group, DC. (2017, February 16). *The. health benefits of cilantro.* Global Healing. https://explore.globalhealing.com/health-benefits-of-cilantro/

Dupuis, A. (2022, September 7). Hydroponic produce: What the foodies are saying. *Eden Green Technology.* https://www.edengreen.com/blog-collection/hydro ponic-produce-what-the-foodies-are-saying

The Editors. (2023, June 17). *Earth Day 2024: How to celebrate Earth Day.* Almanac. https://www.almanac.com/content/earth-day-date-activities-history

Emily. (2020, January 30). *Roasted red pepper soup—creamy, healthy and delicious.* Inside the Rustic Kitchen. https://www.insidetherustickitchen.com/roasted-red-pepper-soup/

Esdaile, G. (2021, June 21). *Finnish blueberry pies.* Delicious. https://www.delicious.

com.au/recipes/finnish-blueberry-pies-recipe-mustikkapiirakka/7n74ev5z?r= recipes/collections/2v0n44e4

Evan. (2015, July 6). *Fresh water greens: A hydroponic success story.* The Urban Vertical Farming Project. https://urbanverticalproject.wordpress.com/2015/ 07/06/fresh-water-greens-the-success-story/

Farris, E. (2023, April 27). *Sautéed kale with garlic and olive oil.* Food & Wine. https:// www.foodandwine.com/recipes/sauteed-kale-with-garlic-and-olive-oil

4 types of hydroponics. (2016). GreenCoast Hydroponics. https://www.gchydro. com/pdf/GreenCoast%20Hydroponics-IS-H2O-0501-4%20Types%20of% 20Hydroponics.pdf

Fuller, T. (n.d.). *Thomas Fuller > Quotes.* GoodReads. https://www.goodreads.com/ author/quotes/433477.Thomas_Fuller

Goldsmith, S. (n.d.). *Strawberry lemonade.* BBC Good Food. https://www.bbcgood food.com/recipes/strawberry-lemonade

Greeley, S. (2020. February 19). *12 quotes about the joy of cooking from the heart.* Little Rae's Bakery. https://littleraesbakery.com/2020/02/19/12-quotes-about-cooking-from-the-heart/

Hansen, K. (2020, April 29). 12 stars cultivate green thumbs during the pandemic. *Architectural Digest.* https://www.architecturaldigest.com/story/celebrities-gardening-while-stuck-at-home

Harley, S. (2016, March 2). *Vegetable lasagne.* Delicious. https://www.delicious. com.au/recipes/summer-vegetable-lasagne-even-hardened-carnivores-love/ 2a2315b3-ddeb-4927-ab12-c9c9c01d4bdf

Harper, S. (2018, June 13). *The greenhouse where tomatoes grow in Iceland.* Atlas Obscura. https://www.atlasobscura.com/articles/farms-in-iceland

Harris, Kim. "32 Inspirational Gardening Quotes." Tree Hugger. https://www.tree hugger.com/inspirational-gardening-quotes-4868813

Heidi. (2022, September 1). *How to make arugula pesto.* FoodieCrush. https://www. foodiecrush.com/how-to-make-arugula-pesto/

Hodgson Burnett, F. (n.d.). *Frances Hodgson Burnett quotes.* AZ Quotes. https:// www.azquotes.com/author/2192-Frances_Hodgson_Burnett

Hoidal, N., Reardon, A., Worth, L., & Rogers. M. (n.d.). *Small-scale hydroponics.* University of Minnesota Extension. https://extension.umn.edu/how/small-scale-hydroponics#pots-and-substrate-2644461

Hu, S. (2021a, August 9). *Tomato and mozzarella caprese salad.* Ahead of Thyme. https://www.aheadofthyme.com/40-best-salad-recipes/

Hu, S. (2021b, August 16). *Grilled shrimp salad.* Ahead of Thyme. https://www. aheadofthyme.com/grilled-shrimp-salad/

Hu, S. (2021c, October 25). *Chicken garden salad with ranch dressing.* Aheadofthyme. https://www.aheadofthyme.com/2016/03/grilled-chicken-garden-salad-with-homemade-ranch-dressing/

Hu, S. (2021d, October 29). *The perfect Greek salad.* Ahead of Thyme. https://www.aheadofthyme.com/2016/03/the-perfect-greek-salad/

Hu, S. (2022a, May 7). *Caesar salad.* Ahead of Thyme. https://www.aheadofthyme.com/caesar-salad/

Hu, S. (2022b, May 18). *Italian pasta salad.* Ahead of Thyme. https://www.aheadofthyme.com/italian-pasta-salad/

Hu, S. (2022c, August 22). *Classic coleslaw.* Ahead of Thyme. https://www.aheadofthyme.com/classic-coleslaw/

Hydroponic systems & what's right for you. (2019, July 24). *HydroPros.* https://hydropros.com/blogs/growers-corner/6-types-hydroponic-systems

Hydroponics market size, share & trends analysis report by type (aggregate systems, liquid systems), by crops (tomatoes, lettuce, peppers, cucumbers, herbs), by region, and segment forecasts, 2021–2028. (n.d.). Grand View Research. https://www.grandviewresearch.com/industry-analysis/hydroponics-market

Irene, W. (2015, January 21). *Earthy potato chive soup [vegan].* One Green Planet. https://www.onegreenplanet.org/vegan-recipe/potato-chive-soup/

Jagdish. (2021a, April 10). *Growing herbs hydroponically.* Agri Farming. https://www.agrifarming.in/growing-herbs-hydroponically-farming-practices

Jagdish. (2021b, November 17). *Top 15 vegetables to grow in hydroponics.* Gardening Tips. https://gardeningtips.in/top-15-vegetables-to-grow-in-hydroponics

Jagdish. (2022, February 22). *Common mistakes made in hydroponic farming.* Agri Farming. https://www.agrifarming.in/common-mistakes-made-in-hydroponic-farming-things-to-avoid-for-beginners

Johnson, L. (2018a, June 1). *Best light for plant growth.* EZ Gro Garden. https://ezgrogarden.com/commercial-growing/best-light-for-plant-growth/

Johnson, L. (2018b, July 25). *Why use hydroponics?* EZ Gro Garden. https://ezgrogarden.com/hydroponics/why-use-hydroponics/#:

Jones, J. (n.d.). *Judith Jones > Quotes.* GoodReads. https://www.goodreads.com/author/quotes/437416.Judith_Jones

Joy. (2021a, March 16). *Female dragon plant profile.* RayaGarden. https://www.rayagarden.com/garden-plants/female-dragon-profile.html

Joy. (2021b, September 9). *Chinese money plant profile.* RayaGarden. https://www.rayagarden.com/garden-plants/chinese-money-plant-profile.html

Joy. (2021c, September 9). *Philodendron profile.* RayaGarden. https://www.rayagarden.com/garden-plants/philodendron-profile.html

Joy. (2021d, September 18). *Arrowhead vine profile*. RayaGarden. https://www.raya garden.com/garden-plants/arrowhead-vineprofile.html

Joy. (2021e, October 29). *Peace lily profile*. RayaGarden. https://www.rayagarden. com/garden-plants/peace-lily-profile.html

Joy. (2021f, November 1). *Devil ivy profile*. RayaGarden. https://www.rayagarden. com/garden-plants/devil039s-ivyprofile.html

Leclerc, A. H. (n.d.). *The Kratky method: A brilliant hydroponics setup you need to know*. Garden & Happy. https://gardenandhappy.com/kratky-method/

Lemon balm information. (n.d.). Mount Sinai. https://www.mountsinai.org/health-library/herb/lemon-balm#:

Leonard, C. (2021, February 17). *Spider plants are hardy hydroponic plants—this is how they grow best*. HappySprout. https://www.happysprout.com/inspiration/growing-spider-plants/#:

Lisa. (2021. October 29). *20+ beautiful plants that grow in water*. RayaGarden. https://www.rayagarden.com/garden-design/plants-that-grow-in-water.html

LookWhatsCooking. (2023, September 14) *Buttery garlic green beans*. Allrecipes. https://www.allrecipes.com/recipe/230103/buttery-garlic-green-beans/

MacDonald, J. (2017, August 7). *What is natural lighting?* Full Spectrum Solutions. https://www.fullspectrumsolutions.com/pages/what-is-natural-lighting#:

Mattson, N., & Daughtrey, M. (2022, January 1). *Common diseases of hydroponic leafy greens and herbs*. E-Gro. https://e-gro.org/pdf/E701.pdf

McHugh, S. (2023, May 31). *The 10 best grow lights of 2023, tested and reviewed*. The Spruce. https://www.thespruce.com/best-grow-lights-4158720

Merriam-Webster. (n.d.-a). Germinate. In *Merriam-Webster.com dictionary*. Retrieved June 21, 2023, from https://www.merriam-webster.com/dictionary/germinate

Merriam-Webster. (n.d.-b). Herb. In *Merriam-Webster.com dictionary*. Retrieved June 25, 2023, from https://www.merriam-webster.com/dictionary/herb

Merriam-Webster. (n.d.-c). Hydroponics. In *Merriam-Webster.com dictionary*. Retrieved May 22, 2023, from https://www.merriam-webster.com/dictionary/hydroponics

Merriam-Webster. (n.d.-d). Sustainable. In *Merriam-Webster.com dictionary*. Retrieved July 19, 2023, from https://www.merriam-webster.com/dictionary/sustainable

Meyer, P. J. (n.d.) *Paul J. Meyer quotes*. BrainyQuote. https://www.brainyquote.com/quotes/paul_j_meyer_393225

Montapert, A. A. (n.d.). *Alfred A. Montapert quotes*. BrainyQuote. https://www.brainyquote.com/quotes/alfred_a_montapert_109332

Neveln, V. (2015, June 9). Learn to graft your favorite plants. *Better Homes &*

Gardens. https://www.bhg.com/gardening/yard/garden-care/how-to-graft-plants/

NoSoilSolutions. (n.d.). *5 pieces of advice for hydroponic beginners.* https://www.nosoilsolutions.com/advice-for-hydroponic-beginners/

O'Donnell, D. (2022, November 7). *Why dissolved oxygen is important in hydroponics.* Sensorex. https://sensorex.com/2022/11/07/dissolved-oxygen-hydroponic-systems/

O'Donnell, D. (2023, March 1). *6 types of hydroponic systems explained.* Sensorex. https://sensorex.com/2019/10/29/hydroponic-systems-explained/

Okafor, J. (2022, December 18). *69 plant quotes to inspire your green thumb and plant love.* Trvst. https://www.trvst.world/environment/plant-quotes/

Parish, S. (2016, October 5). *No-meat broccolini balls.* Delicious. https://www.delicious.com.au/recipes/no-meat-broccolini-balls-october/qyQm65cN

Penney, J. C. (n.d.). *James Cash Penney quotes.* BrainyQuote. https://www.brainyquote.com/quotes/james_cash_penney_226503

Pentz, C. M. (n.d.). *Croft M. Pentz quotes.* AZ Quotes. https://www.azquotes.com/author/47544-Croft_M_Pentz

Prasanniya. (2022, May 29). *Do grow light colors matter?* Hydroponic Way. https://hydroponicway.com/do-grow-light-colors-matter

A quick guide to growing herbs indoors—hydroponically. (2016, May 24). *Foody.* https://foodyverticalgarden.com/blogs/resources/127149763-a-quick-guide-to-growing-herbs-indoors-hydroponically

Quinn Davies, K. (2015, October 3). *Apple and blueberry crumble with roasted almond and peanut topping.* Delicious. https://www.delicious.com.au/recipes/apple-blueberry-crumble-roasted-almond-peanut-topping/85f33256-7104-435e-bd9d-3cfc250f25f2?current_section=recipes

Quinn, H. (2016, February 1). *Green frittata.* Delicious. https://www.delicious.com.au/recipes/green-frittata/4D7ndylQ

Riley, P. (n.d.). *Pat Riley quotes.* BrainyQuote. https://www.brainyquote.com/quotes/pat_riley_147924

Robinson, B. (2019, August 26). What are hydroponic systems and how do they work? *Fresh Water Systems.* https://www.freshwatersystems.com/blogs/blog/what-are-hydroponic-systems

Sánchez, E., Ford, T., Di Gioia, F., & Flax, N. (2023, May 1). *Hydroponic systems and principles of plant nutrition: Essential nutrients, function, deficiency, and excess.* Penn State Extension. https://extension.psu.edu/hydroponics-systems-and-principles-of-plant-nutrition-essential-nutrients-function-deficiency-and-excess#:

Shiffler, A. (2019, September 12). *Vermiculite: Uses for growing plants, safety, and comparison to Perlite*. Herbs at Home. https://herbsathome.co/what-is-vermiculite/

Somers, S. (n.d.). *Suzanne Somers quotes*. BrainyQuote. https://www.brainyquote.com/quotes/suzanne_somers_674411

Srivastava, J. K., Shankar, E., & Gupta, S. (2010). Chamomile: A herbal medicine of the past with a bright future. *Mol med report, 3*(6), 895–901. 10.3892/mmr.2010.377

Stanchfield, D. (n.d.). *Darby Stanchfield quotes*. BrainyQuote. https://www.brainyquote.com/quotes/darby_stanchfield_915007

Stella & Simon. (2023, January 12). *Hydroponic greenhouse—Build from scratch, or buy a kit?* Backyard Garden Lover. https://www.backyardgardenlover.com/hydroponic-greenhouse/

Trebuchet03. (2022, June 13). *Hydroponics—At home and for beginners*. AutodeskInstructables. https://www.instructables.com/Hydroponics---at-Home-and-for-Beginners/

Trees.com Staff. (2023a, March 22). *The Kratky method—Grow food the passive hydroponic way (step by step guide)*. Trees.com. https://www.trees.com/gardening-and-landscaping/the-gratky-method

Trees.com Staff. (2023b, April 13). *Hydroponic growing media 101—The ultimate guide*. Trees.com. https://www.trees.com/gardening-and-landscaping/growing-media

Vanzile, J. (2022, June 24). *How to grow and care for dragon tree (Dracaena Marginata) indoors*. The Spruce. https://www.thespruce.com/grow-dracaena-marginata-indoors-1902749#:

von Braun, W. (n.d.). *Science quotes*. BrainyQuote. https://www.brainyquote.com/quotes/wernher_von_braun_107615?src=t_science

Wattage calculator—How much light should you have? (n.d.). Organica Garden Supply. http://www.organicagardensupply.com/grow-lights/wattage-calculator-how-much-light-should-you-have/#:

Webb, S. (2023, April 28). *Can Dracaena grow in water? A guide to hydroponic care*. Garden's Whisper. https://gardenswhisper.com/can-dracaena-grow-in-water/

WebMD Editorial Contributors. (2020, August 24). *Health benefits of basil*. Nourished by WebMD. https://www.webmd.com/diet/health-benefits-basil

Weintraub, P. G., Recht, E., Mondaca, L. L., Harari, A. R., Diaz, B. M., & Bennison, J. (2017). Arthropod pest management in organic vegetable greenhouses. *Journal of integrated pest management, 8*(1). https://doi.org/10.1093/jipm/pmx021

White, A. (2022, March 31). *Plant nutrients: What they need and when they need it.*

Gardener's Path. https://gardenerspath.com/how-to/composting/plant-nutrients/

Wickison, M. (2023, July 6). *25 of the best plants for indoor hydroponics*. Dengarden. https://dengarden.com/gardening/indoor-hydroponic-garden

Wood, P. (2017, February 13). *Spiced eggplant fritters*. Delicious. https://www.delicious.com.au/recipes/spiced-eggplant-fritters/OsDqG4jc

Zimmern, A. (2023, May 18). *Cold cucumber soup with yogurt and dill*. Food & Wine. https://www.foodandwine.com/recipes/cold-cucumber-soup-yogurt-and-dill

IMAGE REFERENCES

Bereberdina, E. (2022, May 22). *Aeroponic plant for growing plants* [Image]. iStock. https://www.istockphoto.com/photo/aeroponic-plant-for-growing-plants-seedlings-of-green-lettuce-sprouts-in-pots-under-gm1398150831-452382078

Cepris. (2016, February 17). *Pots for hydroponics* [Image]. Pixabay.com. https://pixabay.com/photos/plant-hydroponic-growth-1204662/

Lilkin. (2018, March 29). *Set of aeroponic and hydroponic plant growth systems* [Image]. https://www.istockphoto.com/vector/hydroponic-and-aeroponic-growth-systems-gm938985886-256751935

MAKY_OREL. (2019. February 10). *Germination dicotyledon* [Image]. Pixabay. https://pixabay.com/illustrations/germination-dicotyledon-plant-seed-3989959/

Mor Shani. (2023, February 14). *Net pots* [Image]. Unsplash. https://unsplash.com/photos/a-group-of-plants-that-are-sitting-on-a-table-fth2H_a1-tQ

Stambaugh, K. (2023a, June 12). *Prompt: Chrysanthemums hydroponic* [AI-generated Image]. Midjourney (v. 5.2). https://www.midjourney.com

Stambaugh, K. (2023b, June 12). *Prompt: Deep water culture hydroponics* [AI-generated Image]. Midjourney (v. 5.2). https://www.midjourney.com

Stambaugh, K. (2023c, June 12). *Prompt: Ebb and flow hydroponics* [AI-generated Image]. Midjourney (v. 5.2). https://www.midjourney.com

Stambaugh, K. (2023d, June 12). *Prompt: Flowers* [AI-generated Image]. Midjourney (v. 5.2). https://www.midjourney.com

Stambaugh, K. (2023e, June 12). *Prompt: Nutrient film technique* [AI-generated Image]. Midjourney (v. 5.2). https://www.midjourney.com

Stambaugh, K. (2023f, June 12). *Prompt: Wick system* [AI-generated Image]. Midjourney (v. 5.2). https://www.midjourney.com

Stambaugh, K. (2023g, June 20). *Coco coir* [Photograph].

Stambaugh, K. (2023h, June 20). *Deep water culture buckets* [Photograph].

Stambaugh, K. (2023i, June 20). *Fan supplies for the hydroponic garden* [Photograph].

Stambaugh, K. (2023j, June 20). *Hydroponic nutrients* [Photograph].

Stambaugh, K. (2023k, June 20). *Indoor grow tent* [Photograph].

Stambaugh, K. (2023l, June 20). *Supply of micronutrients* [Photograph].

Stambaugh, K. (2023m, June 20). *Testing supplies for hydroponics* [Photograph].

Stambaugh, K. (2023n, June 21). *Lights, growing mediums, and germination supplies* [Photograph].

Stambaugh, K. (2023o, June 21). *Prompt: Hydroponic orchids* [AI-generated Image]. Midjourney (v. 5.2). https://www.midjourney.com

Stambaugh, K. (2023p, June 21). *Prompt: Kratky method* [AI-generated Image]. Midjourney (v. 5.2). https://www.midjourney.com

Stambaugh, K. (2023q, June 29). *Prompt: Vertical hydroponic system* [AI-generated Image]. Midjourney (v. 5.2). https://www.midjourney.com

Tropical Borneo. (2022, September 30). *Mustard pakcoy or sawi sendok in hydroponic farming* [Image]. iStock. https://www.istockphoto.com/photo/brassica-rapa-mustard-pakcoy-or-sawi-sendok-in-hydroponic-farming-photo-with-blurred-gm1424060690-468896122

Williams, P. (2023a, June 29). *Cafe in a hydroponic greenhouse in Iceland* [Photograph].

Williams, P. (2023b, June 29). *Iceland hydroponic greenhouse* [Photograph].

Williams, P. (2023c, June 29). *Iceland hydroponic greenhouse tomatoes 1* [Photograph].

Williams, P. (2023d, June 29). *Iceland hydroponic greenhouse tomatoes 2* [Photograph].

Made in the USA
Columbia, SC
26 April 2024

bf1b4362-e40f-4a86-83d9-c0cb95aeeeb4R01